T0213116

SpringerBriefs in Computer Science

More information about this series at http://www.springer.com/series/10028

Tatiana Galibus • Viktor V. Krasnoproshin
Robson de Oliveira Albuquerque
Edison Pignaton de Freitas

Elements of Cloud Storage Security

Concepts, Designs and Optimized Practices

Tatiana Galibus
Belarusian State University
Minsk, Belarus

Viktor V. Krasnoproshin
Belarusian State University
Minsk, Belarus

Robson de Oliveira Albuquerque
University of Brasília
Brasília, Brazil

Edison Pignaton de Freitas
Federal University of Rio Grande do Sul
Porto Alegre, Brazil

ISSN 2191-5768   ISSN 2191-5776   (electronic)
SpringerBriefs in Computer Science
ISBN 978-3-319-44961-6   ISBN 978-3-319-44962-3   (eBook)
DOI 10.1007/978-3-319-44962-3

Library of Congress Control Number: 2016955170

Printed on acid-free paper

This Springer imprint is published by Springer Nature
The registered company is Springer International Publishing AG
The registered company address is: Gewerbestrasse 11, 6330 Cham, Switzerland

Abstract

This book is a result of scientific and industrial collaboration in the field of cloud protection. It provides guidelines for the practical implementation of security architecture in a particular corporate cloud. The authors are mathematicians and specialists in data modeling and security. The scientific collaboration with the industry inspired the authors to attempt to conceptualize the common processes and strategies in cloud security in order to make the security system deployment as simple and transparent as possible. The deployment is broken in several essential steps that allow splitting the functionality of the security architecture of any cloud into a set of modules. The first step is the level of architecture where the authentication and key establishment procedures are identified. The second step provides the support of the authorization and other additional security mechanisms for each component of the cloud. The continuous verification of security support on all levels (data, processes, and communication channels) allows avoiding the common security breaches and protecting against the most dangerous attacks at maximum. Additionally, it is proposed to perform the optimization of the selected set of mechanisms in order to intensify the efficiency of the security system.

Preface

Cloud-based systems are gaining importance due to the number of companies that are adopting them as the IT support for their core activities. With this increase in the number of cloud users, the visibility of these systems is also increasing, which calls the attention of cybercriminals to expend time trying to attack them. The goal of these criminals is to have access to valuable data of individual or corporate users. In this context, the cloud security is an important current issue in IT. The list of problems related to cloud security is large [1], inheriting all sorts of network attacks usually performed against corporate servers, but it also includes brand new types of attacks tailored to the new cloud environment. However, in the other end, IT security professionals are working hard to create solutions for these problems, which makes the list of solutions as big as the list of problems or even larger [2].

The Cloud Security Alliance (CSA), an organization that promotes the best practices for providing security assurance within cloud computing, provides a list of problems and currently available countermeasures, besides those that are being developed. The list of problems released by CSA in March 2016, known as the "Treacherous 12" [3], describes the 12 top security threats organizations face in the cloud computing environment. The problems covered by this list summarize the concerns about cloud security organizations have to care about. Its goal is to present knowledge about the most important problems so that companies can prevent them and properly get the benefits of cloud computing, without incurring in the drawbacks raised by the possible vulnerabilities.

Despite an active community sharing information about the problems organization may face in the cloud environment, an important problem is still an absence of a strategic approach in this field to face these problems. In other words, a practitioner, i.e., an IT security professional, incurs the risk to become lost among the several possible methods of protection. In light of this fact, it is possible to state that there is a clear need for a straightforward guide able to provide an understanding of the placement and the need for specific security mechanisms. The basic set of questions asked by these professionals is as follows:

1. How to implement a security system for a cloud? This is a very general question, which in fact involves several others. The very first one is related to the type of the cloud that it is taken into concern, i.e., which is the adopted cloud model (private, public, hybrid, community)? What is the volume of data stored in this cloud? Are there confidentiality concerns? If so, in which level? What are the possible threats and vulnerabilities a given company must care about? In summary, before trying to answer the main question about how to implement a security system for a given cloud, there is a need for a well-defined characterization of the cloud environment and the involved risks that specific cloud will face. Only after this characterization is it possible to start thinking about a concrete implementation of a security system.

2. Where to start? Okay, the IT personnel in charge of the cloud security have done the characterization of the cloud environment that has to be secured and started thinking about its implementation. However, where should they start? Which part of the cloud should be handled and in which order? Is there any requirement to be considered beforehand?

3. How to select the necessary mechanisms? From the myriad of available security mechanisms that can be adopted, which one should be selected and why? Which one is the most suitable? Informed decisions must be taken, and after taken, they have to be justified.

4. How to verify that the system is optimal? Mechanisms are finally selected and implemented, that's all? Not at all! How to verify the adopted security solution is optimal? This concerns not only the optimality in terms of covering all identified possible threats and vulnerabilities but also in allowing the system perform its activities without performance degradation due to the security mechanisms' overhead.

5. How to verify its security? Fine, the security system was finally implemented covering the requirements presented by the characterization, taking into account performance issues and other concerns. At this point in time, personnel in charge of the security can rest, right? Unfortunately, the answer is a sounding no! After all the work that was done, the security team has to perform exhaustive penetration tests. They have to check every possible breath that may still exist, as well as be diligent and continuously verify if the adopted security solution is really the most suitable one.

It is possible to conclude that in the field of cloud security, there is a demand for specific practice-oriented models. Such models should help practitioners to understand the cloud environment they have to protect, what are the alternatives they have to implement this protection, and how to verify that a given adopted alternative is really the most suitable one. Understanding this need, this book approaches the problem of cloud security in a concrete and straightforward way. It proposes a transparent protection system model based on a cryptographic approach that can be easily verified for security requirements. The proposal is based on a modular approach, i.e., on a set of interdependent mechanisms oriented toward solutions for specific tasks. The modular structure of a proposed model allows adjusting and optimizing the system according to the required needs. This means that it is able to scale according to the size of the cloud, but also is able to tackle specificities of the different types of cloud models. Additionally, the book answers the question about how to start by proposing an iterative two-step method of constructing a security system for a cloud environment.

The advantages of the proposed approach are transparency, adjustability, and the systematic construction. This allows adapting the solution for different needs, providing a step-by-step method to build up and run a security system for clouds.

With the aim to address the abovementioned topics, the content of this book is pedagogically organized in order to facilitate the readers' understanding. Following this principle, the book is structured as follows:

The first chapter presents the current cloud storage landscape. It describes the basic types of cloud from the point of publicity as well as the important characteristics concerning security. The main concepts and characteristics of cloud-based systems are also revisited in order to provide a comprehensive background to the reader. The chapter describes the main processes, components, and services of the cloud storages. The chapter also discusses a set of requirements for the cloud system life cycle and the appropriate set of requirements for cloud security system. These requirements provide the basis for a specification of the goals of a cloud protection system.

The second chapter classifies the basic vulnerabilities and attacks on the cloud. The types of attacks are specified according to the type of cloud, component, and process, and the vulnerabilities are also specified according to the component or process. The chapter formulates the basic security problem for the cloud, i.e., the set of security requirements for the security system in the cloud. The details provided in this chapter complement to more generic and high-level ones discussed in the previous chapter.

The third chapter specifies the basic mechanisms of the security system. It gives the definitions and the strategies in mobile security, authentication and key distribution, authorization, and threat intelligence. The mechanisms are specified in accordance with attacks they neutralize. This chapter is organized so that the reader can easily refer to the definition and basic functionality of a specific mechanism and go further on the details, according to his/her needs.

Finally, the last chapter provides the practical recipe to solve the security problems that affect cloud storage systems. It contains the best practices and their analysis from the point of security and optimization. As it was highlighted above, it is important to analyze the suitability of a given security solution, not only in terms of how well it addresses a given security problem but also in terms of the overhead it imposes to the system. This aspect refers to the suitability of the security solution under consideration. An illustrative example is provided in order to make clear for the readers how to address the studied security problems. This example describes a practical solution to protect cloud storage, referring to the detailed content presented through the book content.

Minsk, Belarus   Tatiana Galibus
                                                                         Viktor V. Krasnoproshin
Brasília, Brazil   Robson de Oliveira Albuquerque
Porto Alegre, Rio Grande do Sul, Brazil   Edison Pignaton de Freitas

References

1. US Department of Defense. Department of Defense Cloud Computing Security Requirements Guide, Version 1, Release 2, 18 March, 2016
2. Cloud Security Alliance.
3. Cloud Security Alliance. "The treacherous 12 – cloud computing top threats in 2016" Available online:https://downloads.cloudsecurityalliance.org/assets/research/top-threats/Treacherous-12_Cloud-Computing_Top-Threats.pdf

Contents

Chapter 1
Cloud Environment Security Landscape

Cloud computing is a trend in the Internet-based computing, providing on-demand shared processing and data storage resources to remote computing devices. It is able to empower resource-scarce devices to provide end users highly demanding applications, enabling access to data and sophisticated software services virtually anywhere. It provides on-demand access to a shared pool of configurable computing resources, such as application servers, storage servers, networks, and services. These resources can be quickly provisioned and released, requiring a minimal management effort. All these features allow end users and companies to rely on third-party computing services paid according to the resources usage, which leads to economic and operation advantages, as they can focus in their core tasks and pay for just the used services.

Despite the great benefits provided by cloud-based computing services, as it relies on connectivity, network access, and data distribution, a number of security issues are raised, both for corporate and for private users. In order to better understand the risks, the threats and the associated attacks to the cloud computing and storage services providers, it is mandatory to revisit the way these services are offered and organized. This chapter provides a comprehensive overview of the cloud computing and storage landscape, trying to conclude about the main security issues and requirements to be observed in this area.

1.1 Cloud Computing Model Background

Despite a number of technologies that grow around the concept of cloud computing and storage, the key aspect that supports the idea behind it is the business model known as *pay as you go*. According to this business model concept, the user pays just for what it effectively used, such as pay-per-view TV channels that charge the users by the individual TV programs, films, or sport matches they watch. Another

© The Author(s) 2016
T. Galibus et al., *Elements of Cloud Storage Security*, SpringerBriefs in
Computer Science, DOI 10.1007/978-3-319-44962-3_1

key idea brought from the business area to compose the cloud computing idea is the *self-service* model. The users request services as and when they need them.

From the technological perspective, the key concepts that support these business models that inspired the conception of the cloud computing are the virtualization and the offer of open APIs. The first represents the basis for cloud computing as the virtualization provides means to perform efficient resource sharing. Virtualization allows the allocation of resources of the same computer hardware to several users, but maintaining the isolation and independence from each other, which is also known as encapsulation. It also provides means to location abstraction, i.e., the user does not know where exactly his/her applications are effectively running. Moreover, it allows the on-demand resource allocation. The second, i.e., open APIs, allows an easy mechanism to access the offered services and at the same time facilitates the integration of these services with other applications and solutions that may be used as components or building blocks.

According to cloud computing definition published by NIST [1], there are five essential characteristics that are related to the cloud computing, described as follows:

- On-demand self-service: A user can request and automatically have access to computing capabilities, as processing or storage resources, according to his/her needs, without any interaction with the service provider.
- Broad network access: The computing capabilities are available over the network and can be accessed by standard mechanisms. Any kind of client platform may access them, as long as it has access to the network, independent of how power-ful it is.
- Resource pooling: The provided computing resources are pooled in order to serve multiple users. According to the users' demands, physical and virtual resources are dynamically assigned and reassigned to fulfill the current demands. This fact is associated to location independence, which states that the user has no control of the exact location of the accessed resource. Higher level abstractions are offered, such as the choice to access resources located in a given country or state, for instance.
- Rapid elasticity: The accessed capability can be rapidly provisioned and released, according to the current demands. From the users' perspective, the resources are "virtually" unlimited and can be provisioned at any quantity and at any time.
- Measured service: The access to the cloud resources is measured, i.e., their usage is monitored, controlled, and reported, providing transparency about the amount of the used services for both the service providers and consumers.

Besides the five essential characteristics, the NIST cloud computing definition also lists three cloud service models and four deployment models, as can be observed in the schematic presentation of the NIST definition depicted in Fig. 1.1.

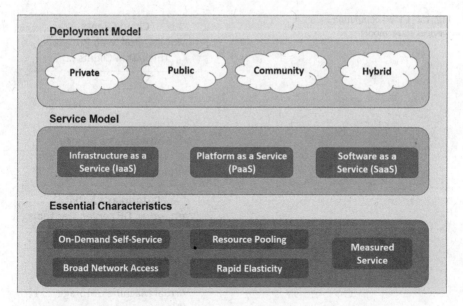

Fig. 1.1 Schematic presentation of the NIST definition of cloud computing elements

1.2   Cloud Service Models

The service models described in the NIST definition follows a service-oriented architecture approach, which proposes that everything in a system is a service, defining three classes of provided services, namely: Infrastructure as a Service (IaaS), Platform as a Service (PaaS) and Software as a Service (SaaS). These classes of services are organized in a stack as presented in Fig. 1.2.

These three service layers can be explained as follows:

Infrastructure as a Service (IaaS) As the position of the IaaS showed in Fig. 1.2 suggests, this is the most basic cloud service model. Providers of IaaS offer virtual machines, storage service, and network services, among other fundamental computing resources. The IaaS refers to online services that abstract the user from the details of the underlying infrastructure, such as physical location, physical computing resources, load balancing, data partitioning, security mechanisms, backup, and recovery support, among others. The consumer does not manage or control the underlying cloud infrastructure, but has control over operating systems, storage, and limited control over given resources, such as a firewall. The virtual machines are run by a hypervisor, such as VMware ESX/ESXi, Xen, Oracle VM, or KVM. These hypervisors form pools within the cloud operational system, allowing the support for large numbers of virtual machines and the ability to scale services up and down according to changes in customers' demands. Another alternative is the usage of Linux containers, which run in isolated partitions of a single Linux kernel. This kernel runs directly on the physical hardware. In order to isolate the Linux kernel,

Fig. 1.2 Cloud computing
services stack model

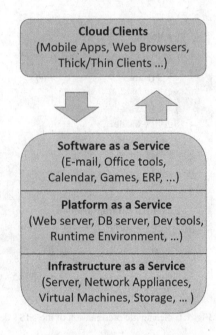

cgroups and namespaces are used, providing security and container management features. The use of containers offers higher performance than virtualization, because they do not need hypervisors, thus avoiding their associated overhead. Another benefit in using containers is the fact that they dynamically auto-scale with the demanded computing load, which eliminates the problem of over-provisioning and enables an efficient usage-based billing, an important feature to the self-service characteristic of cloud computing. IaaS cloud providers supply their offered resources on demand, i.e., according to the clients' current demands, from their large pools of equipment installed in their data centers. Cloud clients use the provided IaaS services by deploying their operating systems images and applications in this provided infrastructure. They are responsible for maintaining these operating systems and application software, as this is not part of the IaaS offered service. The IaaS billing is done on a utility basis, i.e., the costs refer to the amount of resources effectively allocated and used by the cloud client. Some important aspects to be observed in the billing process are the compliance with service level agreements (SLAs) and observing specific quality of service (QoS) requirements, which is very common specially when network resources are part of the contracted services.

Platform as a Service (PaaS) PaaS providers offer environments of application development to their customers. The provider typically develops toolkits and standards for application development and channels for distribution and service payment. The "package" delivered by the PaaS cloud providers generally includes an operating system, a programming-language execution environment, a database, and a web server. The customers of PaaS suppliers can develop and run their software systems on the contracted cloud platform without concerning about the complexity of managing the underlying hardware and software layers, besides the reduced cost, as they do not need to buy this underlying infrastructure. It is common that the provided PaaS solutions offer the automatic scaling of the underlying computer and storage resources to match application demands, so that the cloud user does not have to bother in allocating resources manually. Integration and data management solutions are also commonly provided services. An example is the Integration Platform as a Service (iPaaS), which enables customers to develop, execute, and control integration flows, driving the development and deployment of integrations without installing or managing any hardware or middleware [2]. Another example is the Data Platform as a Service (dPaaS), which delivers integration and data management solutions as a fully managed service [3]. Under the dPaaS model, it is the PaaS provider that manages the development and execution of data solutions by building tailored data applications for the customer, which is freed from this management task. However, the users retain transparency and control over data through visualization tools. In PaaS model, consumers do not manage or control the underlying cloud infrastructure, i.e., the underlying network, servers, operating systems, or storage, but they have control over the deployed applications and possibility to access configuration settings of the environment that hosts their applications.

Software as a Service (SaaS)   The Software as a Service (SaaS) providers offer their users access to application software and databases. These cloud providers manage all the necessary underlying infrastructure and platforms to run the applications. The SaaS model is also referred to as "on-demand software" and is usually priced on a pay-per-use basis or using a subscription fee. SaaS cloud providers install and operate application software in the cloud and the users access the software from cloud clients. These clients can be thin or thick clients, mobile apps, or browsers, for instance. Cloud users do not manage the cloud infrastructure nor the platform in which the applications run, which simplifies maintenance and support, as they do not need to install and run the application on their own computers. There is an important difference between cloud applications compared to other applications in their scalability. This difference is due to the fact that cloud application can rapidly scale up by cloning tasks onto multiple virtual machines during run-time to meet changing demands [4]. This is achieved by load balancers that distribute the work over the set of virtual machines of the service provider, which is a process completely transparent to the cloud user. A large number of cloud users can be served at once as any machine may serve more than one cloud user, according to the current demands. The pricing model varies, but a common way to charge for SaaS applications is typically a monthly or yearly flat fee, which may be per user or group of users, allowing scaling and adjustments in cases in which users are added or removed. The SaaS model has the potential to reduce IT operational costs by outsourcing hardware and software maintenance and support to the cloud service provider. This enables the business to concentrate efforts and financial resources in their core tasks, instead of spending money in IT operations and hardware/software expensive updates and maintenance. Another advantage is that with the applications centrally hosted, updates can be released easier. An important drawback of SaaS model is related to the users' data that is stored on the cloud provider's database servers. This drawback is related to two possible problems, i.e., information privacy and accessibility. SLAs related to SaaS provision usually have specific clauses to handle these issues, which gain more importance as the numbers of software solutions based on SaaS grow.

1.3 Deployment Models

The deployment models refer to the way the cloud systems are implemented. There are two main models, the private and the public ones, and two other main variations, the hybrid and the community ones. It is also possible to name other minor variations, but the abovementioned four types are the main types described in the literature. Figure 1.3 illustrates these possible types of cloud.

Interesting to notice in Fig. 1.3 is the highlight of important aspects related to the cloud deployment, in which the first is related to the place where the cloud is deployed, for instance, inside an organization (on premises) or external/outside the organization (off premises). The second important aspect is particularly related to the community clouds, which refers to the interests or concerns that identify a given community, and thus the associated cloud, as it will be further explained. Moreover, possibility of interconnections among clouds is also illustrated. In the following, the description of each deployment model is presented:

Private Private clouds are operated exclusively for a given organization. It may be managed internally, by a third party, or a combination of them. It may be hosted either internally (on premises) or externally (off premises). The adoption of a pri-

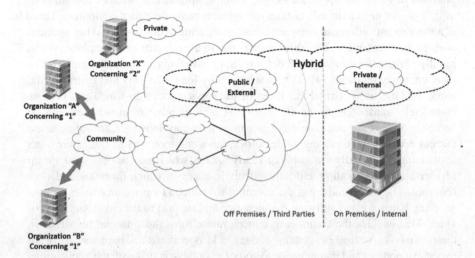

Fig. 1.3 Cloud deployment models

vate cloud can improve business, but every step in the evolution of its life cycle raises security issues that must be addressed to prevent serious vulnerabilities. An important issue in this context is the access of the business cloud-based services by mobile devices of the company's employees. Another issue to be considered before adopting this model is the trade-off between the permanent investments which update the infrastructure and return the cloud provides to the company.

Public Public clouds are those in which the services are offered to the open public. They may be free or charged per use. They may be offered either by private companies, universities, governmental organizations, or even combinations of them, and they exist on the premises of their providers. Security concerns are in general substantially different for services (applications, storage, and other resources) provided by public clouds if compared to those offered by private clouds, starting from the assumption that they operate over non-trusted networks.

Community Community cloud shares infrastructure between several organizations from a specific community with common concerns or interests (policy, security concerns, compliance, jurisdiction, mission, etc.). It may be managed internally or by a third party and either hosted in or off premise. The costs are spread over the members of that community that supports the common concern. Figure 1.3 presents an example in which organizations "A" and "B" share a common concern "1" and they support a community cloud related to this concern. Conversely, organization "X" has other concerns and does not share the community cloud, but it has its own private cloud. The security aspects related to community cloud vary much depending on the type of concern shared by the organizations that support a given community cloud.

Hybrid Hybrid cloud is a composition of two or more types of clouds (private, community, or public) that remain distinct entities, but are bound together by standardized or proprietary technology that enables data and application portability. They offer the benefits of multiple deployment models. The hybrid deployment model allows the extension either of the capacity or the capability of a cloud service, by aggregating, integrating with another cloud service, or customizing the provided service. A great variety of hybrid cloud composition can be built. For example, an organization may store sensitive client data on premise on a private cloud, while offering a business intelligence application on a public cloud off premise. Another typical example of hybrid cloud composition is of a private cloud that having a huge demand takes resources from a public cloud to increase its computing capacity and respond to the current growing demand. The adoption of a given hybrid cloud depends on a number of factors such as data security and compliance requirements. Regarding the security, this is a major concern specially when sensitive data is under concern.

1.4   Cloud Storage Classification

Cloud storage provides a very convenient and highly flexible way of storing data with access to it from different device locations.

The basic features of cloud storage that can be highlighted are:

- Availability – the ability to access the data when it is needed.
- Durability – this feature refers to how sustainable and how protected from crashes the storage is.
- Performance – this feature refers to the speed of the data access.

The basic functions of the cloud storage are backup, synchronization, and sharing of the files that compose the data storage. The first deals with the ability to create and manage copies of the data that can be recovered in case of need. The second deals with the consistency management of distributed copies of the same data, while the third refers to the ability in sharing the data among different computers.

In order to support these functions, any of the service or the deployment models (see Sects. 1.2 and 1.3) can be adopted. Cloud storage is convenient and cost-effective but has the certain security concerns. The risk that information can be accessible by unauthorized users is rather high.

The service and the deployment models of cloud storages follow the general models of cloud services and deployment models. They can be of different types of cloud storages, dividing the security concern between the client organization and the service provider as follows:

- SaaS model: In the SaaS model, the cloud storage is based on the external provider. The user or organization does not have the complete control of the data. The security is the responsibility of provider.
- IaaS model: In IaaS model, the cloud storage provider sets up the infrastructure, i.e., the basic components. The control is shared between organization and provider and the security is supported by the trusted authority, the organization, or both.
- PaaS: In the PaaS model, the highest level of centralization and security control is adopted.

Table 1.1 summarizes the security responsibility distribution.

The cloud storages can also be private, community, or public.

The recommendation for the public cloud users is rather simple. The security of data is the users' responsibility and they have the control over the data. A user should take care of the data confidentiality by setting up strong password, configuring two-factor authentication (see Sect. 3.1), and using at least AES encryption (see Sect. 3.2).

The community cloud provides limited access to a certain group of participants and therefore has elements of access control. The responsibility of the data is shared between users and organizations.

Table 1.1 Summary of the security responsibility distribution, according to the different types of cloud storage service model

Service model	Centralization level	Security control
SaaS	Low (data controlled by provider)	By provider
IaaS	Middle (data control is shared)	Shared between provider and organization
PaaS	High (data controlled by organization)	It is mainly the responsibility of the organization

Table 1.2 Summary of the security responsibility distribution, according to the different types of cloud storage deployment model

Deployment model	Centralization	Security
Public	Decentralized	User controlled
Community	Partly centralized	Shared between user and community
Private	Centralized	Organization controlled

The private cloud is completely centralized and the responsibility of data security is entirely to the organization. Table 1.2 summarizes the security concern according to the deployment model.

1.4.1   Corporate Cloud Storage Types

In the corporate and enterprise environment, the security requires special attention and more precise control [5]. Therefore, the general service and deployment models require modifications. Due to the presence of confidential and probably highly secure data in the organization, it is not recommended to use the SaaS service because of the high probability of security leak.

For highly sensitive data, it is important to either adopt a secured storage service (IaaS model) or deploy the native infrastructure with the local server of the organization's ownership (in premises) in order to provide the sufficient security level (PaaS model). Using the software of an external provider is not recommended due to the absence of control of secured data.

If the confidentiality level is very high (at least three levels of security in organization) or if the corporation is big and has sufficient resources, it is preferable to use PaaS model and deploy its own storage service based on secured provider platform.

The deployment model suitable for the corporate cloud is only private due to the presence of one common control center.

Another concern is that with the adoption of cloud services, the data moves outside the protected security perimeter. That is why the processes connected to the data transfer and the client device protection should be properly organized. It is recommended to keep mobile devices and client protection at the highest possible level, i.e., encrypt the data on clients and on mobile devices. Another option is that data leaving the premises can be kept open once its security level is open [6].

Totally there can be several storage types based on confidentiality levels and the security perimeter options:

- IaaS: only two levels of confidentiality. Security perimeter is high and medium.
- PaaS: any levels of confidentiality. Security perimeter is high, low, and medium.

1.4.2   Corporate Cloud Storage Components

The basic components of the cloud storage are:

- The server: The server that can support all the data processing and encryption functions and also store the data. These functions (data processing storing and securing) can be separated into several servers, but it is recommended to keep one secure center because the enhanced centralization increases security.
- The client: The client supports the communication with the cloud. The protection architecture on a client device should be carefully designed as it has limited resources and cannot support high level encryption or key generation in most of the cases. At the same time, the possibility of breaking into an organization via client device is much higher than that via server.
- The mobile device: Mobile devices are considered separately because they can leave the premises of the organization; they can be stolen and they have very limited protection resources. Therefore, the protection model of mobile device requires special attention.
- Channels: Channels are simply data transfer procedures. Obviously, in the cloud environment, the channels are considered unprotected and sending information within security perimeter should be supported by encryption.

The storage channels serve the following functions:

- Sending data to client
- Synchronizing share list with client
- Getting modified data from client

The channels connected to information protection are:

- Sending keys to client
- Sending user credentials to server

Processes:

- The processes in the storage include the security processes, monitoring and maintaining the data integrity, consistency, and availability. Backup and re-encryption are also part of the processes.

1.4.3 Centralization Features

The corporate cloud storage security differs from that of a public cloud as the organization is responsible for it.

The importance of centralization and consolidation for the business solutions is an acknowledged fact [7].

Therefore:

- The user keys are generated on a server (encryption server). There is no private key in organization.
- The control of data security is passed to a server.
- The storage processing and encryption functions are performed by one authorized center.
- The service model is PaaS as in other scenarios the complete control of the data center is difficult to achieve.
- The data access policies are managed in a centralized manner.
- The storage is maintained in a virtualized manner to increase consolidation and simplify control.

The centralized storage strategies are as follows [7]:

- *Network-attached storage (NAS)* – multiple app servers simultaneously connect to centralized storage servers with replication and failover.
- *Storage area network (SAN)* – redundant array of disks seen as a local volume by the servers attached to it, for high availability and faster disk I/O performance than NAS, a virtualization cluster for providing intensive access.
- *High-availability cluster* – contains not just file storage and database servers but also application servers. Traffic is distributed by a load balancer.

1.4.4 Basic Scenarios

For the purpose of this book (the practically oriented security analysis and implementations), it is necessary to select several most common cloud security system deployment models that are applicable to different corporate cloud types [8, 9]. It was decided to construct and provide detailed guidelines in the three basic scenarios:

- Small company
- Medium company
- Big company

Each of these scenarios supports a different security level and therefore a different set of mechanisms.

For a small company, a basic security without complex access policies is provided. It is considered that manual setting of access control is enough so the number

Table 1.3 Security levels according to the size of companies

Size of company	Number of people	Resources	Security
Small	<20	Limited	Acceptable
Medium	<100	Sufficient	Optimized
Big	>100	Excessive	Best possible

of people accessing the data should not be more than 20. Otherwise it is difficult to manage and support the security of such system. It is adopted that such system has only two levels of confidentiality and does not have a complex structure of file sharing to be accessed so that the groups of users that can access the sets of documents can be directly configured.

For a medium company, a more complex scenario is applied. The automated access control method is recommended as the number of people grows up to 100. In order to manage the key revocation situations (i.e., a user leaves the organization), it is necessary to monitor and to provide sufficient control to such situations. Besides that, it is necessary to organize a constant monitoring in such cloud as it is more difficult to provide a centralized control. The ways the keys are distributed also should be stronger due to the fact that such infrastructure is more vulnerable than the previous one, uses a greater number of mobile devices, so the security perimeter is vaguer. This scenario can be adopted in most companies. It was implemented as IaaS in Storgrid protected cloud [10].

The big company scenario assumes that a company has enough resources and a skilled developer team in order to implement the most high-end secured practices. Besides the complex protection mechanisms, it requires sufficient network velocity within the organization. The company size is more than 100 and adopts the three or four confidentiality levels, i.e., document protection levels. It supports the complex access policy and allows controlling the user attributes automatically.

These three scenarios meet the compromise of resources and security at different levels. They may be not completely implemented at each company, but they should use the most adoptable security components from each scenario. Table 1.3 summarizes this discussion about the security levels according to the size classification of the companies.

1.5   Cloud Security Requirements

Despite the number of benefits to cloud computing, concerns about security still hinder its massive adoption in many sectors that require a very high level of control and/or security. An example of sector in which security concerns around cloud computing continues to be a major issue is the financial services sector. Observing the sensitivity of data handled by this sector and the regulated environment in which most financial service providers operate, IT solutions to address their needs must be sure that any data exposed on the cloud is effectively protected. A number of other examples of data-sensitive sectors can be mentioned, such as e-health, e-government, and homeland defense, among many others.

Observing the importance security has for data computing systems in many domains, this concern is seriously considered in the cloud-based systems arena. Observing the major security goals, i.e., confidentiality, integrity, and availability, it is possible to conceive major cloud security requirements that have to be observed by organizations desiring to implement the usage of cloud-based systems in their operations. Still considering security in general, any security consideration for cloud-based systems should adhere to the following guidelines determined by the above three major security goals, as follows:

Confidentiality Data confidentiality is the property of preserving authorized restrictions on information access and disclosure, including means of protecting personal privacy and proprietary information. This assures that data contents are not made available or disclosed to illegal users. In the cloud environment, outsourced data stored in a cloud is out of the owners' direct control, thus measuring to guarantee that only authorized users can access the sensitive data, while others, including cloud service providers, should not gain any information about the data they handle. While data owners must have full access to the stored data and the cloud-provided services, no leakage of the data contents to other users may occur.

Integrity Data integrity assures protection against improper information modification or destruction and includes ensuring information, non-repudiation, and authenticity. It demands maintaining and assuring the accuracy and completeness of data. The data in a cloud has to be stored correctly and trustworthily, meaning that it should not be illegally or improperly modified, deliberately deleted, or maliciously fabricated or faked. It also requires means for auditability, so that in case any undesirable operations corrupt or delete the data, the owner should be able to detect the occurrence of these events.

Availability Data availability states that the legitimate user has access to the desired data whenever he or she desires. It ensures that data continues to be available at a required level of performance in any situation, implying means for data recovery in case of disastrous events.

Consideration on security concerns related to cloud-based systems must be taken into account considering the different service model categories described in Sect. 1.2, i.e., Infrastructure as a Service (IaaS), Platform as a Service (PaaS), and Software as a Service (SaaS), as each model brings different security requirements and responsibilities. A direct effect of this fact is an additional security goal, besides the confidentiality, the integrity, and the availability, that even being related to them gains a similar status due to the fact that many cloud-based systems use off premise resources, thus requiring a strict data access control, which can be detailed as follows.

Access Controllability   The goal of the access controllability is that the data owner can perform the selective restriction of access to his/her data outsourced to cloud. Legal users can be authorized by the owner to access the data, while others cannot access it without permissions. It is highly desirable that fine-grained access control mechanisms to the outsourced data can be implemented. This mechanism should allow the data owner setup grants for different users with different access privileges regarding different parts of the stored data. This access control must be performed only by the owner of the data.

It is important to highlight that in order to assess the security requirements for cloud-based systems, besides the consideration of these above-described high-level security goals and the services models, the deployment models play also an important role in the definition of the specific security requirements for a given cloud-based solution. In order to evaluate these requirements, it is also very relevant to take into account the main threats that cloud-based systems face during their operation. These topics will be further explored in the rest of this chapter.

1.5.1   Top Cloud Security Threats

The Cloud Security Alliance (CSA) released in March 2016 the "Treacherous 12" [11], a list with the top security threats organizations face when using cloud services. According to this list, the top security threats summarizes the concerns about what cloud security organizations have to care about in order to get the benefits of cloud computing, without incurring in the drawbacks raised by the possible vulnerabilities that cloud-based systems have. These 12 top cloud security threats can be summarized as follows:

(a) *Data breaches*: Cloud-based systems face many of the same threats as traditional network-based system solutions, but due to the fact that the volume of stored and processed data is very huge, cloud providers become very attractive for cyber criminals. When data breaches occur, companies may incur fines, or they may face lawsuits or criminal charges; among this huge amount of processed and stored data, there are very sensitive data as intellectual property or personal health information. In such events occurring, severe negative effects, such as brand damage and loss of business, can impact organizations for years. Observing the severity of data breaches, CSA has recommended organizations use multifactor authentication and encryption to protect itself against this threat.

(b) *Compromised credentials and broken authentication*: The causes of data breaches, as well as of other attacks, are in general lax authentication, weak passwords, poor key, and careless certificate management. The user identity management is a common problem faced by organizations as they try to allocate appropriate permissions to the user's job role. However, in many cases, fails occur, such as forgotten removal of user access when a job function changes or a user leaves the organization. The use of multifactor authentication systems such as smart cards and one-time passwords help to protect cloud services as they are difficult for attackers to make use of stolen credentials to log in the cloud system.

(c) *Hacked interfaces and APIs*: Cloud interfaces and APIs are used by cloud clients to manage and interact with the cloud services. The security of the cloud services depends on the security of the cloud interface and APIs as they tend to be the most exposed part of a system due to the fact that they are accessible from open networks, i.e., the Internet. Weak interfaces and APIs expose organizations to security issues related to confidentiality, integrity, availability, and accountability. This is especially important concerning data in transit and data in use. Among the CSA recommendations, to face this kind of threat ranges from secure coding to the performance of exhaustive penetration tests.

(d) *Exploited system vulnerabilities*: The exploitation of software system vulnerabilities is not new, but they became an even more important issue in cloud computing-based systems. The resource sharing among different organizations creates new opportunities that attackers can explore. CSA recommends the usage of best practices to detect possible vulnerabilities and the prompt addressing of the detected problems. This preventive behavior to discover and repair vulnerabilities is small compared to the potential damage attacks may cause.

(e) *Account hijacking*: Cloud-based systems offer new possibilities to be explored by attackers to take control of legitimate users' accounts using ordinary methods, like phishing, fraud, malicious transaction manipulations, or data modification. Attackers may also take legitimate users' account controls to use cloud applications to launch other attacks, like distributed denial of service. CSA recommends the use of multifactor authentication and avoidance of account credentials sharing as possible ways to mitigate this problem.

(f) *Malicious insiders*: The malicious insider motivation can be very diverse, ranging from data theft to revenge. This threat may come from different sources, i.e., the malicious insider may be a current or former employee, a system administrator, a contractor, or a business partner. In a cloud scenario, an insider can destroy whole infrastructures or manipulate data. Systems that depend solely on the cloud service provider for security, such as encryption, are at greatest risk.

The CSA recommends that organizations control the encryption process and keys, segregating duties and minimizing access given to users. Effective logging, monitoring, and auditing administrator activities are also critical.

As the CSA notes, it's easy to misconstrue a bungling attempt to perform a routine job as "malicious" insider activity. An example would be an administrator who accidentally copies a sensitive customer database to a publicly accessible server. Proper training and management to prevent such mistakes become more critical in the cloud, due to greater potential exposure.

(g) *Advanced persistent threat parasites*: This type of threat is classified by CSA as a form of attack that infiltrates cloud systems and stay hidden and persistently performing their nefarious activities for long periods of time. An example that can be mentioned is malicious software that continuously exports valuable private information, such as intellectual property, to malicious users off premises.

Their activity is hidden by blending the malicious traffic in the normal one, thus making it difficult to be detected. They normally access the cloud by breaths like phishing, portable media infected with malware, or direct attacks against the cloud.

(h) *Permanent data loss*: Permanent data loss is a vulnerability that any cloud provider shares with any other data center facility, due to events such as natural disasters. With the enhancement of the cloud providers' practices, permanent data is becoming rarer. Malicious users may perform an attack permanently deleting data, but mechanisms to avoid this possibility are more mature and well disseminated nowadays, such as different levels of backup, data distribution, and the adoption of best practices in business continuity and disaster recovery. Besides the role of the cloud provider in avoiding malicious users permanently deleting data, cloud clients have also their role in this matter. Once encrypted data is uploaded to the cloud, if by any reason the user loses the key, the data encrypted with that key is also lost. Thus, key management plays an important role in relation to possible permanent data loss.

(i) *Inadequate diligence*: When subscribing cloud services, organizations may be diligent in order to avoid incurring in risks that may be present in different forms, i.e., technical, financial, commercial, compliance, or legal. Before moving toward a cloud-based solution, the organization has to understand these risks and consider whether or not they are acceptable and what can be done to address them. A typical problem faced by many organizations is lack of technical competence in the development team due to underestimation of the complexity involved in the cloud adoption process. Another common problem is failing in scrutinizing a contract to understand and be aware of the provider's liability in case of data loss or service interruption.

(j) *Cloud service abuses*: Cloud services can be used to perform malicious activities, such as DDoS attacks, sending spam and phishing emails, and hosting malicious content, or used to conduct a brute force attack to break keywords. Cloud providers have to be able to detect this type of abuse in the use of the cloud provided resources, so that they can be stopped. Providers need to allow their customers to report abuse because even if the customers are not the direct prey of a given malicious activity, the abuse of the cloud services delivered to a given customer may incur in service degradation, for instance, when a contracted processing resource has been used to break a keyword instead of doing what it was supposed to do or even in data loss in worst case scenarios.

(k) *DoS attacks*: With the growth in the use of cloud-based systems, DoS attacks gained more popularity as it concerns the service availability. DoS attacks can slow down or just completely suspend services and the user has no alternative than to wait until the response is provided or the service is reestablished. Another important aspect related to DoS attacks is that the cost in terms of processing power or the bandwidth that a DoS attack consumes ends up in the bill the cloud consumer has to pay.

(l) *Shared technology, shared dangers*: Cloud providers share infrastructure, platforms, and/or applications, depending on the cloud service model. In case vulnerability arises in any of these layers, it affects everyone sharing the corresponding resources. Simple errors or mistakes performed in the cloud infrastructure may compromise the entire cloud. This is an important concern to the cloud consumers, which make many organizations consider twice before moving to a cloud-based solution.

1.5.2 Cloud Security Requirements Recommendation

In light of the above-described threats, some key recommendations can be provided to organizations that are considering the adoption of a cloud-based solution, as well as to cloud provider companies. These recommendations can be summarized as follows:

(a) *Adoption of a defense-in-depth strategy*: This strategy includes host-based and network-based intrusion detection systems, multifactor authentication on all hosts, patching shared resources, applying the concept of least privilege, and network segmentation.

(b) *Well-defined plans*: In case "the worst" happens, there is an important need for a continuity and recovery plan, with well-defined actions and responsibilities, as well as the resources to be used in the performance of these actions. Another important plan is related to attack mitigation, i.e., acting before the attack effectively occurs. This plan may be able to allow administrators to have access to resources when they need them, which avoid, for instance, DoS attacks, by preventing valuable resources to remain locked by malicious software.

(c) *Adequate diligence*: When contracting cloud services, organizations have to be diligent in scrutinizing contracts, considering risks, and evaluating the pros and cons of different aspects related to the adoption of a given cloud-based solution. They also have to be aware of the potential risks that they may face in the future.

(d) *Strict usage regulations*: The organization contracting cloud services is also responsible for the cloud security in the sense that their employees may perform misuse of the offered resources or may put in risk the system by adopting not suitable or not recommended behaviors, such as using portable media that may be contaminated with malicious software or overusing a given resource unnecessarily. Use regulations have to be well defined and be strict to protect the cloud environment.

(e) *Staff control*: Besides the strict usage regulation, organizations are recommended also to control their users' activities by controlling the encryption process and key management, segregating duties, and minimizing access given to them. On the cloud provider side, administrator activities should be audited and effective logging and monitoring have to be performed. Proper training to prevent unsuspecting mistakes is also important as minor mistakes may result in great potential exposure in the cloud environment. Human resources departments play an important role in this aspect in the moment an employee is hired.

(f) *Best practices adoption*: Simply adopting the best practices in terms of IT process, the organizations can mitigate a number of risks. These practices include regular vulnerability scanning, prompt patch management, and quick follow-up on reported system threats, among many others. Systems administrators have to be aware of the current practices and be updated about the latest vulnerabilities and the respective countermeasures.

(g) *Security-focused software development*: As any other software, software developed for the cloud environment have to be developed taking into account security concerns. This means that the code development has to address quality patterns that avoid the exploitation of vulnerabilities such as stack overflow or malicious data handling. Threat modeling for applications and systems, including data flows, architecture, and design, is an important part of the development life cycle, conducting to a security-focused development. Extensive code reviews and rigorous penetration testing are also important and must take place.

References

1. Mell P, Grance T (2011) The NIST definition for cloud computing. National Institute of Standards and Technology, Gaithersburg, September 2011
2. Pezzini M, Lheureux BJ (2011) Integration platform as a service: moving integration to the cloud, Gartner
3. Lawson L (2016) IT business edge. Available online: http://www.itbusinessedge.com/blogs/integration/liaisons-data-platform-as-a-service-includes-data-mapping.html
4. Hamdaqa M, Livogiannis T, Tahvildari L (2011) A reference model for developing cloud applications. In: Proceedings of the 1st international conference on cloud computing and services science, pp 98–103
5. Chen D, Zhao H (2012) Data security and privacy protection issues in cloud computing. Computer Science and Electronics Engineering (ICCSEE), 2012 international conference on, Hangzhou, pp. 647–651
6. Cloud Security Alliance. Security guidance for critical areas of cloud computing https://cloud-securityalliance.org/research/security-guidance/
7. http://blog.iweb.com/en/2015/04/benefits-centralized-storage/14645.html
8. Marston S, Li Z, Bandyopadhyay S, Zhang J, Ghalsasi A (2011) Cloud computing – the business perspective. Decis Support Syst 51(1):176–189
9. Gupta P, Seetharaman A, Raj JR (2013) The usage and adoption of cloud computing by small and medium businesses. Int J Inf Manag 33(5):861–874
10. Storgrid: www.storgrid.com
11. Cloud Security Alliance (2016) The treacherous 12 – cloud computing top threats in 2016 Available online: https://downloads.cloudsecurityalliance.org/assets/research/top-threats/Treacherous-12_Cloud-Computing_Top-Threats.pdf

Chapter 2
Common Cloud Attacks and Vulnerabilities

Technological and advanced systems, such as cloud computing, suffer different kinds of attacks, be it a small, medium, or large cloud solution provider. In fact, the size of the cloud provider does not avoid it from suffering a cyber attack. Most of these attacks are common and already identified by security experts, while other attacks can be considered new in the perspective of how they are applied and what they can achieve in cloud systems.

It is true that cloud security has evolved through recent years. Advances in cryptography are applied to cloud solutions; the application of best security practices and security measures in distributed systems is an example of such advances, even though big security problems in cloud solutions still exist with the necessity of solutions, both practical and theoretical. Thus existing security problems make cloud users victims of attacks where data and information can be lost, changed, or stolen. Considering such assumptions, below are some examples of attacks and vulnerabilities that affect cloud solutions.

2.1 Types of Attacks in Cloud Systems

There are many different kinds of attacks and threats applied to cloud systems. Some of them are possible just because there is a cloud solution. Others are considered variations of common attacks, with the difference that they are applied to the computational resources available to cloud solutions and cloud users. Below there is a brief description of the known attacks applied to cloud providers and solutions, be it small, medium, or large [1–12].

Denial of Service
Basically denial of service (DoS) makes resources unavailable to users [4, 6]. Normally it is expected to be a high impact in such attacks because many users consume cloud resources; thus the damage is likely to be very high.

© The Author(s) 2016
T. Galibus et al., *Elements of Cloud Storage Security*, SpringerBriefs in
Computer Science, DOI 10.1007/978-3-319-44962-3_2

DoS attacks are characterized by the exhaustion of resources due to the high overload the cloud component demands when under attack. Services can be flooded by abuse of protocol vulnerabilities or significantly increasing the amount of requests to cloud pages of files, thus consuming processing power and bandwidth, which affects the physical infrastructure as much as the virtualized components, such as memory and CPUs.

Sometimes, when the cloud provider tries to work against the attacker, i.e., by providing more computational power, actually to some point, it even supports the attacker by enabling him to do more damage on a service's availability, starting from a single entry point. In this case, the attacker does not have to flood a single target (i.e., a single server or a single IP address), but he has to flood a single cloud service address to achieve a full unavailability of the system.

Distributed Denial of Service

Distributed DoS (DDoS) is considered a variation of DoS attacks. It has the same points of evaluation, but it has more entities engaged in the attack; thus the amount of traffic generated grows exponentially.

DDoS attacks aim at exhausting device infrastructure resources to cause service disruption and hence its unavailability. This is done in a distributed fashion, where different entities send large amount of data to be processed in the cloud provider.

Considering its volumetric approach, DDoS attacks basically consist of sending a large number of requests that either overwhelm services, in which several nodes send traffic in a coordinated way, resulting in higher attack efficiency, and more complex mitigation given to the one who coordinates the attacks normally is obfuscated.

DDoS and DoS attacks can be organized in two major classes: volumetric attacks and by protocol abuse. Protocol abuse covers low-volume, slow-rate attacks where legitimate traffic probes exploiting specific protocol features, characteristics, or implementation details lead to exhausting some of the victim's resources, and consequently legitimate requests are not properly responded. Volumetric attacks, on the other hand, include attacks where large traffic volumes flood the victim, exceeding its processing capacity or link bandwidth, so that legitimate requests are not treated.

Amplified Reflection DDoS

Amplified reflection DDoS (AR-DDoS) is considered a volumetric attack, where it can be divided in flooding attacks and amplified reflection attacks. Both forms try to overload some victim resource, usually bandwidth, by sending large traffic volumes to the victim.

In flooding attacks, compromised entities send traffic straightforward to the victim, while in reflection attacks, intermediate entities, named reflectors, are used to flood the victim. For the purposes of the attacker, a reflector is any entity that sends a response to a request previously received.

Normally reflectors of interest are those that amplify, i.e., their response produces more volume than the original input. This behavior is characterized by a reflection factor, indicating how much traffic the reflector generates. Basically with amplification attack, the reflector potentializes generated traffic to make resources unavailable.

It is important to point that AR-DDoS is appealing for attackers because it requires much less effort when compared to other forms of DDoS, where nodes have to be, either manually or through the use of malware, compromised in preparation for attack. In the case of AR-DDoS, attackers need only identify nodes that are vulnerable for reflexion, usually due to misconfiguration. In the attacker's perspective, identifying possible reflector is easy by using automated scripts and programs, which by their turn are trivially modified to execute attacks.

Malware Injection

Cloud solutions allow users to read and write files in virtual file system at will. Most of the time, an ordinary user only needs a regular account and he can upload as many files as the available space in the cloud provider permits him to do so. In such cases, attackers can also upload malware to cloud file systems and thus trick users to download and execute them [4–7]. As malware can be embedded in a large number of different file types, attackers may be able to bypass cloud security solutions, as they are limited to few file types. In this case there is degrade in the detection coverage process. Moreover, exporting binaries or every sort of file to the cloud for investigation cannot be considered a good approach because it may create a point of failure by flooding the cloud with benign binaries.

More advanced possibilities consist of attackers manipulating service instances in cloud solutions. Considering service manipulation perspective, an attacker can control a virtual machine to any particular purpose he wishes, ranging from data modifications through eavesdropping. Normally this kind of attack requires the creation of cloud modules such as Software as a Service (SaaS), Platform as a Service (PaaS), or Infrastructure as a Service (IaaS) and trick the cloud provider to believe it is part of a normal service offered by the cloud solution. If he succeeds, the cloud provider redirects user requests to the attacker service; thus code is deployed to users to achieve whatever the attacker's intention is.

Theft of Service

Theft-of-service attack uses vulnerabilities in the scheduler of some hypervisors [5]. This kind of failure may allow an attacker to obtain cloud services at the expense of others. Basically, this attack is conducted when the hypervisor uses a scheduling mechanism, which fails to detect and properly account information of usage of resources by poorly behaved virtual machines.

Since the hypervisor is responsible for schedules and also in managing virtual machines, vulnerabilities in the hypervisor scheduler may result in inaccurate and unfair scheduling. Thus, an attacker can gain advantage in the system by never scheduling its processes in scheduling ticks. This way an attacker uses the cloud provider resources (storage system or OS platform) for a long period without representing it in a billing cycle.

Authentication Abuse

Authentication is considered a vulnerable point in cloud providers [7]. Many cloud solutions still use a username/password mechanism to authenticate its users. Also, poor implementation of authentication leads attackers to easily gain control over accounts of users in cloud environments. There is a huge list of techniques and technologies used to steal passwords, attack password systems, and circumvent authentication security.

Basically such attacks attempt to exploit the authentication process to verify the identity of a user, service, or application. These types of attacks include brute force, where an attacker repeatedly tries to guess user name and password by using an automated process of trial and error; insufficient authentication, where an attacker accesses a web service containing sensitive content or functions without having to properly authenticate with the system; and weak password recovery validation, where an attacker is able to access a service that provides him the ability to illegally obtain, change, or recover other passwords of users.

Side-Channel

A side-channel attack (SCA) is any attack based on information gained from the physical implementation of a system, rather than brute force or theoretical weaknesses of the system [6, 7]. Information gained such as timing information, power consumption, electromagnetic leaks, acoustic data, differential faults, data reminisce, or row hammer can provide an extra source of information, which can be exploited to break the system.

SCA in cloud solutions happen when hardware leaks information of use to a potential attacker; thus he attempts to compromise the cloud solution by placing a malicious virtual machine in close convenience to a target cloud server system and then debut a SCA so he can obtain extra information to complete the attack using other methods to gain control of the system or to disrupt its activities. SCA exist for IaaS, SaaS, and PaaS types of cloud providers.

To be effective, some SCA require technical knowledge of the internal operation of the system and details of how it is implemented.

Wrapping

Wrapping attacks are conducted during the translation of SOAP messages between a legitimate user and the web server [1, 4]. This attack uses XML signature wrapping (or XML rewriting) to exploit a weakness when web servers validate signed requests. By duplicating the user's account and password in the login period, the attacks can embed bogus element into the message structure, moves the original message body under the wrapper, replaces the content of the message with malicious code, and then sends the message to the server.

Since the original body is still valid, the server will be tricked into authorizing the message that has actually been altered. As a result, the attacker is able to gain unauthorized access to protected resources and execute his commands in the system as he wishes.

Since most cloud users normally request services from cloud computing service providers through a web browser, wrapping attacks can cause damage to cloud systems as well, and the attackers could take unprivileged actions on victim's accounts in cloud providers.

Stepping-Stone

In stepping-stone, attackers try to achieve their objectives while avoiding revealing their identities and locations to minimize the possibility of detection and attribution [9].

Normally, this kind of attack is accomplished by indirectly attacking the targeted victim through a sequence of other hosts (stepping-stones). Such hosts can be obtained in illegal botnets (included for hire), where a bot master can set up command and control server and stepping-stones into cloud providers with objectives such as to steal sensitive information or to gain unauthorized access to cloud resources to make it behave abnormally.

Account/Service Hijacking

An attacker gaining access to an account can manipulate and change the data and therefore make the data untrustworthy [8, 9]. Following this perspective, any attacker having access to a virtual machine hosted in cloud providers with business systems in it can include malicious code into this system to attack users. If an attacker controls the environment, he can also disrupt the service by turning off services, rendering it inaccessible in the perspective of the users.

Man-in-the-Middle

Man-in-the-middle (MITM) attack is carried out when an attacker places himself between two entities [6, 8]. Anytime attackers can place themselves in the communications path, there is the possibility to secretly relay and alter the communication between two parties who believe they are directly communicating with each other.

MITM attack is also a kind of attack that allows active eavesdropping. The attacker makes independent connections with the victims and relays messages between them to make them believe they are talking directly to each other over a private connection, when in fact the attacker controls the entire conversation. In such cases, the attacker must be able to intercept all relevant messages passing between the two victims and inject new ones. MITM attacks are used in many circumstances, including in cloud communication processes.

Ransomware

Ransomware is a type of attack supported by malicious application that steals control of the user's machine or data, or it may lock the system's screen or lock user's files and then demands a payment from the user to restore normal access to the ransomed content or system [13].

Some ransomware will encrypt files, so the user can't access it normally without a decryption key. This type of malware is normally named crypto-ransomware.

Considering a cloud perspective, if the user stores his files in a synchronized folder in the cloud and falls victim of a ransomware that encrypts his files, then in a synchronization process, all devices can overwrite files with encrypted versions of it leading the user to a full loss of his data. Still in a cloud perspective, if ransomware gains control over cloud infrastructures (OS or virtual machines), it can take control of the infrastructure, which can lead to a full stop of cloud services.

Man-in-the-Cloud

Man-in-the-cloud (MITC) attacks rely on common file synchronization services [14, 15]. Such services can use the synchronization services for hosting techniques used for command and control (C&C), data exfiltration, or remote access (or all of them together). One of the problems of this attack is that it is not easily detected by ordinary security measures. In this kind of attack, the attacker gets access to the victim's account even without compromising the victim's credentials.

MITC does not require any particular malicious code or exploit to be used, while the use of well-known synchronization protocols makes it extremely hard to differentiate normal traffic from malicious traffic. It basically requires acquiring the token credentials used by most cloud storage systems and targets users with a phishing attack so the initial steps of the attack can be conducted and the attacker gets the synchronization token.

Once the attacker has the synchronization token, it enables the attacker to share the victim's file synchronization account; thus it permits to access files and infect them with malware. In a normal process, these files will be synchronized by the victim's client application, thus being infected with malicious code.

Phishing

Phishing is a kind of attack where there is an attempt to access personal information from users through social engineering techniques [7]. It is commonly carried out by sending links of web pages in emails or through instant messages or attached files infected with malware or exploits.

It is rather difficult for ordinary users to correctly identify a phishing attack because the information the user receives appear to be correct, leading to a legitimate site for verification. But instead of it, the attack leads users to fake locations. Through this deception, the attacker can obtain sensitive information such as user credentials.

Phishing attack campaigns can be hosted in sites on cloud providers by using cloud services, thus leading attackers to hijack accounts and services in the cloud through traditional social engineering techniques.

SQL Injection

Attackers may explore vulnerabilities of poor implementations of applications in web services and inject a malicious code in order to bypass authentication controls and have unauthorized access to backend databases, thus valuable third-party information.

If this attack is successful, attackers can manipulate the contents of the databases, retrieve confidential data, remotely execute system commands, or even take control of the web server for further activities.

Cross-Site Script
It occurs when a cloud application sends a page containing user-supplied data to the browser without validation, filtering, or escaping. In such cases, attackers inject malicious scripts into a vulnerable dynamic web page to execute in the victim's web browser.

Cross-site scripting (CSS) allows attacks to steal credentials, execute arbitrary code, manipulate session data, or even force download of content in the victim's environment.

Targeted Shared Memory
Attackers may take advantage of shared memory (cache or main memory) of both physical and virtual machines, in which it can lead up to several different types of attacks.

In such cases, attackers can get unauthorized access to information that reveals the internal structure of the cloud. This information may vary, but it can reveal details such as the number of processes running or the number of users logged-in in a specific time or the temporary cookies residing in memory.

2.2   Classification of Attacks According to General Security Mechanisms

After the most common attacks were shortly detailed, Table 2.1 presents a general classification of attacks and which security property it affects.

Cloud providers suffer from different vulnerabilities that can be used to carry out different kinds of attacks. Some types of vulnerabilities are not exclusive to cloud solutions, but any attacker with the correct means can explore them. Below there is a brief description of common vulnerabilities applied to cloud solutions [1, 5, 6, 8, 9, 14].

Virtual Machine Coresidence
Coresidence means that multiple independent clients share the same physical infrastructure. Concretely, virtual machines belonging to different clients may be placed in the same physical machine. Throughout coresidence, security issues, such as cross-VM attack or malicious system administrators, can be explored to interfere in a normal cloud environment and operations.

Table 2.1 Types of vulnerabilities in cloud components

Security property	Availability	Authentication	Authorization	Key distribution
Attack				
Denial of service	X	X		X
Distributed denial of service	X	X		X
Amplified reflection DDoS	X	X		X
Malware injection		X		X
Theft of service	X	X		
Authentication abuse		X		
Side channel	X	X		X
Wrapping		X	X	
Stepping-stone		X		
Account/service hijacking		X	X	
Man-in-the-middle		X		X
Ransomware	X			
Man-in-the-cloud		X	X	
Phishing		X		
SQL injection		X		
Cross-site script		X	X	
Targeted shared memory		X	X	

Session Riding

Session riding happens when an attacker is able to steal and use cookies that identify a particular user to a system or application. An attacker might also use cross-site request forgery (CSRF) attacks in order to trick the user into sending authenticated requests to arbitrary web sites to achieve various attacker objectives.

Virtual Machine Escape

In cloud infrastructures, the physical servers run multiple virtual machines on top of hypervisors. An attacker can exploit a hypervisor remotely by using specific vulnerability present in the hypervisor itself; thus a virtual machine can escape from the virtualized sandbox environment and gain access to the hypervisor and consequently all the virtual machines running on it.

Loss of Physical Control

Cloud users may have their data and software solutions outsourced to cloud providers. As a practical result, they lose direct control on the datasets and software and systems. Basically, loss of physical control means that clients are no longer able to resist certain types of attacks. In such cases, data or software may be altered, lost, or even deleted; thus it is very difficult to ensure data/computation integrity and confidentiality with traditional methods in cloud solutions.

Reliability and Availability of Service
There is a common expectation that cloud services and applications always be available, which is one of the reasons for moving data to the cloud. But bad conditions may lead to power outages where services on the cloud may not be up and running 100 % of the time. It is good sense to take a little downtime into consideration.

Unable to Provide Confidentiality
Cloud solutions are not fully able to guarantee confidentiality. Poor cryptography solutions give false impression of safety to users. If cloud users expect confidentiality in cloud solutions they have to apply their own means to safeguard their secrets. Cloud providers can move files from place to place; thus users cannot determine whether their files are in one place or in another or even worse, if unauthorized users had access to it due to the lack of cryptography premises to ensure confidentiality.

Internet Dependency
By using the cloud services, there is a large dependency upon the Internet connection. If the Internet temporarily fails, the clients won't be able to connect to the cloud services. Therefore, business can lose money, because the users won't be able to use services required for the business operation.

Cloud Service Termination
There is a risk of cloud service providers going out of business. Enterprise-level cloud storage provider may unexpectedly end its operations due to lack of funds; thus if users are not able to move their data from one cloud provider to another, they may lose its data with the real possibility of never getting them back again.

2.3   Classification of Vulnerabilities According to General Security Mechanisms

After the most common vulnerabilities were briefly explained, Table 2.2 presents a general classification of attacks and which security property it affects.

2.4   Threats Applied to Cloud Solutions

Besides vulnerabilities that affect cloud solutions, various types of threats may afflict cloud providers and users. There is a short list below [1, 4–7].

Table 2.2 General classification of attacks and the security property affected

Security property	Availability	Authentication	Authorization	Key distribution
Vulnerability				
Virtual machine coresidence	X			
Session riding		X	X	
Virtual machine escape	X	X	X	
Loss of physical control	X	X	X	X
Reliability and availability of service	X			
Unable to provide confidentiality		X	X	X
Internet dependency	X			X
Cloud service termination	X			

Hackable Interfaces and APIs

Almost every cloud provider offers service solutions and applications interface to development. Code developers interact with cloud systems throughout APIs, including solutions for provisioning, management, orchestration, and monitoring.

There is a strong relation between the security and availability of cloud solutions to the security measures of an API. In other words, weak security implementations of interfaces and APIs expose cloud solutions to security issues associated with confidentiality, integrity, availability, and accountability.

Data Breaches

Many threats that trouble cloud environments are the same worries to traditional corporate networks. The fact is cloud solutions have larger amount of data stored than corporate networks; thus it becomes valuable targets.

The sensitivity of data exposed by data breaches has a strong relation to the potential damage it may cause to users and cloud solutions. Financial information, health information, trade secrets, and intellectual property can be devastating in many aspects.

Due to data breaches, cloud providers may apply high fines and face lawsuits or even criminal charges, which, by its turn, demands high costs in business. Indirect consequences, such as brand damages and loss of clients, may impact companies for years.

Malicious Insiders

Insiders have many possibilities [10]. It may be a current employee, a former employee, a system administrator, a contractor, a business partner, etc. Insider's motivations vary from dissatisfaction to data theft. Due to its characteristics and depending on the level of access, an insider can compromise whole systems or manipulate data.

Compromised Credentials and Broken Authentication

Poor implementation of security mechanism normally leads to user's credentials being compromised and authentication issues broken. Cloud solutions may have identity management problems related to user's role. Strong security mechanisms help avoid such problems.

Moreover, development mistakes, such as hardcoding credentials in software code or embedding cryptographic keys in source code or distributing source codes in public repositories, make this problem larger than it should be. User credentials, user roles, and authentications codes and tokens must be well implemented and protected from unauthorized manipulation.

Account Hijacking

Many attacks provide the possibility to compromise as many accounts as the attacker is able to manage. Fraud, software exploits, and phishing campaigns still have high rate of success in cloud solutions. Problems with shared authentication credentials between user and service increase such possibilities.

Attackers with compromised accounts may launch new attacks, eavesdrop on user's activities, manipulate data or information on behalf of the compromised account, control transactions, and many other opportunities the attacker may find promising.

Exploited System Vulnerabilities

Normally, cloud solutions share infrastructure solutions such as memory, databases, file systems, and other resources. Such resources are also in close proximity to one another. System exploitable vulnerability may affect the whole infrastructure, thus leading to data breaches, information loss, stolen information, etc. In cloud solutions this problem seems much bigger because of multitenancy in cloud solutions. All this creates new attack surfaces, which can be explored by attackers.

Advanced Persistent Threats

Advanced persistent threats (APT) have high level of analytic and technical characteristic that creates means of achieving strategic goals using multiple vectors, be it physical, virtual, social, stealthy, or others. APTs are used to establish and keep continuous covert access, as long as the attacker desires, inside a target's infrastructure and performing the attacker's intentions [16].

Through an APT, an attacker may cause damage, delay actions, destroy information, exfiltrate data and information, provoke wrong signals in systems, and change information and system parameters.

An APT seeks its objectives during a long period of time, and it is able to adapt itself to new circumstances, avoids technological defenses, and keeps in constant communication with its command and control system, even using air gap techniques. Also, an APT is capable of advanced exploitation techniques, uses attacks with no proper defensive measures, and may use exploits as starting point of infection.

An APT uses stealthy capabilities so it is not easily detected by common defense perimeter technology. It may change its behavior to bypass detection, may attach itself to another program, and may even alter firmware and device drivers, so it cannot be removed from the infected resource without enormous amount of efforts. Such characteristics make an APT hard to detect; thus creating countermeasures efficiently is also difficult.

Cloud Service Abuse
Cloud services can be abused to support or facilitate computer power to reprehensible activities (e.g., breaking encryption keys). Other activities could be launching DDoS attacks, sending spam, phishing emails, or hosting malicious content.

Permanent Data Loss
Data loss is a threat that affects cloud solutions due to errors or deliberated attacks. Malicious users have been known to permanently delete cloud data to harm businesses. Also cloud data centers are as vulnerable to natural disasters as any facility.

The affliction of preventing data loss is not all on the cloud provider. If a user decides to encrypt its data before uploading it to the cloud and then loses the key, he also loses the data.

Shared Technology
Sharing technology may implicate in sharing dangers because a shared vulnerability represents significant threat to cloud systems. A shared vulnerability that affects any application affects every server hosting this application. The same applies for vulnerabilities that affect infrastructure or platforms. This way, a single misconfiguration or vulnerability can conduct to a compromise across an entire cloud provider.

Inadequate Diligence
Operational and architectural issues may arise if an organization's development team lacks familiarity with cloud technologies as apps are deployed to a particular cloud.

Also, organizations that embrace the cloud without fully understanding the environment and its associated risks may encounter a lot of different types of associated risks.

DoS Attacks
Basically, DoS attacks affect availability. Considering cloud providers, this attack may be much more bigger due to the resources available in cloud systems. Some types of DoS attacks require enormous amount of efforts and collaborative measures to mitigate and try to stop the attack.

2.5   Classification of Threats According to General Security Mechanisms

After the most common threats were briefly detailed, Table 2.3 presents a general classification of threats and which security property it affects.

Table 2.4 gives the reader a short classification of threats, attacks, and vulnerabilities according to the cloud component it affects.

2.6   Adversary Types Related to Cloud Solution Providers

Security threats that affect cloud providers can come from different sources. Cloud providers can be self-interested, malicious, or even untrusted. Cloud providers can deliberately move data that is rarely accessed to a lower tier of storage for financial reasons. Or it may try to hide a data loss incident due to management errors.

On the other hand, a legitimate cloud provider may also face a motivated adversary heavily funded. With such capabilities, this type of adversary may have the ability to compromise multiple cloud data storage servers in different time intervals. Consequently it is able to modify or delete users' data while remaining undetected by a certain period of time. Anyway, below are some types of adversaries a cloud provider may encounter [11, 12].

Table 2.3 Classification of threats and the security property it affects

Security property	Availability	Authentication	Authorization	Key distribution
Threats				
Hackable interfaces and APIs		X	X	
Data breaches		X		
Malicious insiders	X	X		X
Compromised credentials and broken authentication		X	X	X
Account hijacking	X	X	X	
Exploited system vulnerabilities	X	X	X	X
Advanced persistent threats		X	X	X
Cloud service abuses	X	X	X	
Permanent data loss	X	X	X	X
Shared technology	X	X		
Inadequate diligence		X	X	
DoS attacks	X			

Table 2.4 Classification of threats, attacks, and vulnerabilities according to cloud component

Cloud component affected	Server	Client	Mobile	Channels	Processes
Threats					
Hackable interfaces and APIs	X	X	X		
Data breaches	X				X
Malicious insiders	X			X	X
Compromised credentials and broken authentication		X	X		X
Account hijacking	X	X	X		
Exploited system vulnerabilities	X	X	X		X
Advanced persistent threats	X	X	X	X	X
Cloud service abuses	X				X
Permanent data loss	X	X	X		X
Shared technology	X	X	X		
Inadequate diligence	X	X	X		
DoS attacks	X	X	X	X	X
Vulnerability					
Virtual machine coresidence	X			X	X
Session riding	X	X	X		
Virtual machine escape	X				X
Loss of physical control	X			X	X
Reliability and availability of service	X				X
Unable to provide confidentiality	X	X	X		
Internet dependency	X	X	X	X	X
Cloud service termination	X	X	X		X
Attack					
Denial of service	X	X	X	X	X
Distributed denial of service	X	X	X	X	X
Amplified reflection DDoS	X	X	X	X	X
Malware injection	X	X	X		
Theft of service	X	X	X		
Authentication abuse	X	X	X		
Side channel	X			X	
Wrapping	X	X	X		
Stepping-stone	X				X
Account/service hijacking	X	X	X		
Man-in-the-middle	X	X	X	X	
Ransomware	X	X	X		
Man-in-the-cloud	X	X	X		X
Phishing		X	X		
SQL injection	X				X
Cross-site script	X	X	X		
Targeted shared memory	X				X

Weak Adversary

This adversary is interested in small but destructive actions such as corrupting the user's data files stored on individual servers. Once it is comprised, this adversary can adulterate the original data files or introduce its own fraudulent data, thus preventing the user from being able to retrieve the original data.

Strong Adversary

It is the type of adversary who is able to compromise all the storage servers. This adversary can intentionally modify the data files as long as they are internally consistent. It has the skills to move from server to server at will or can create and delete virtual resources because he can manage the infrastructure and also deliberately share private data.

Self-Interested Cloud Provider

Cloud provider can be self-interested, untrusted, or evil. It might move data that is seldom accessed to a lower tier of storage for profit. It may also attempt to hide user's data loss due to management errors or convoluted failures. It may manipulate its servers to create collusion to gain advantage over adversaries. Basically, it is an untrustworthy service provider.

Economically Motivated Adversary

Adversaries are people who have the capability to remain undetected from cloud service providers and compromise a number of cloud data storage servers in different time intervals for a certain period of time. They can manipulate or delete user's data or can corrupt the user's data files and can infect the original data files by modifying or can replace it with their own data to prevent the original data from being retrieved by the user. In worst cases, he can intentionally modify data files of the entire storage server as long as they are internally consistent, i.e., where all servers intrigue together to hide corruption incident or data loss.

Evil Insider

It can be defined as a type of user with a high level of access in the cloud infrastructure and is frustrated with the cloud provider itself. This kind of adversary has authorized access to the network, system, or data. He can intentionally exceed or misuse that access in a manner that negatively affects the confidentiality, integrity, or availability of the cloud system.

Attack Surfaces on Cloud Systems

In general, any cloud environment can be modeled using three single classes: (i) service users, (ii) service instances, and (iii) the cloud provider [2, 3, 7, 9]. Normally, any interaction in a cloud solution is addressed at least by two entities of the classes. For instance, a user requests a service, or a service instance requests more CPU power from the infrastructure system.

Following this perspective, any attack in the cloud environment corresponds into a set of interactions within the three-class model. Thus a user and a service instance

Table 2.5 Attack surfaces

Attack surface	Description
Service-to-user	This is the ordinary server-to-client interface, thus enabling all kinds of attacks that affect usual client-server architectures as well
User-to-service	It is the common environment a client program provides to a server. Attacks to this surface affect browser-based applications, attacks on browser caches, etc.
Cloud-to-service	Basically this attack surface is related to the service instance, which covers all attacks a service instance can run against its cloud provider
Service-to-cloud	It includes any kind of attack a cloud provider can perform against a service running on its infrastructure
Cloud-to-user	It is not easy to be defined because in ordinary scenarios there exists a service between them. But these services are more related to cloud control such as adding new services or requiring more instances of a service already being in use. It is a separate attack surface, but it is similar to the attacks a common cloud service faces from a user's perspective
User-to-cloud	It is related to any type of attack that targets a user and has its origins (be it spoofed or not) at the cloud system

have the very same set of attack vectors that exist outside the cloud (e.g., SQL injection, XSS, DoS, etc.).

Taking such assumptions in consideration, discussing about cloud security means arguing about attacks with the cloud provider among the list of participants. It is not a requirement for the cloud provider to be malicious itself; it may just play an intermediate role in an ongoing attack or a combination of attacks. Basically the attack surfaces are divided as shown in Table 2.5.

References

1. Chou T-S (2013) Security threats on cloud computing vulnerabilities. Int J Comput Sci Inf Technol 5(3):79
2. Sen J (2013) Security and privacy issues in cloud computing. Archit Protoc Secur Inf Technol Infrastruct 1:1–45
3. Gruschka N, Jensen M (2010) Attack surfaces: a taxonomy for attacks on cloud services. IEEE Cloud 8:40–50
4. Mahajan H, Giri N (2014) Threats to cloud computing security. VESIT, International Technological Conference-2014 (I-TechCON)
5. Hashizume K et al (2013) An analysis of security issues for cloud computing. J Int Serv Appl 4.1:1
6. Singh S (2014) Cloud computing attacks: a discussion with solutions. Open J Mob Comput Cloud Comput 1.1:1–8
7. Singh A, Shrivastava M (2012) Overview of attacks on cloud computing. Int J Eng Innov Technol (IJEIT) 1.4:85–97
8. Modi C et al (2013) A survey on security issues and solutions at different layers of cloud computing. J Supercomput 63(2):561–592
9. Khalil IM, Khreishah A, Azeem M (2014) Cloud computing security: a survey. Computers 3(1):1–35

10. Duncan AJ, Creese S, Goldsmith M (2012) Insider attacks in cloud computing. 2012 IEEE 11th international conference on trust, security and privacy in computing and communications, IEEE
11. Singh R, Kumar S, Kumar Agrahari S (2012) Ensuring data storage security in cloud computing. IOSR J Eng 2:12
12. Acharya S, Siddappa M (2016) A novel method of designing and implementation of security challenges in data transmission and storage in cloud computing. Int J Appl Eng Res 11(4):2283–2286
13. Everett C (2016) Ransomware: to pay or not to pay? Comput Fraud Secur 2016(4):8–12
14. Jabir RM et al (2016) Analysis of cloud computing attacks and countermeasures. 2016 18th International Conference on Advanced Communication Technology (ICACT). IEEE
15. IMPERVA – Man in the Cloud (MITC) attacks, hacker intelligence initiative. July 2015 https://www.imperva.com/docs/HII_Man_In_The_Cloud_Attacks.pdf
16. de Oliveira Albuquerque R et al (2015) Leveraging information security and computational trust for cybersecurity. J Supercomput 46:1–35

Chapter 3
Cloud Storage Security Mechanisms

In this chapter, the most applicable cloud storage security mechanisms are introduced. The chapter can be used as a reference to a set of cloud security solutions. The mechanisms are grouped according to the related security task or problem:

- Authentication and tokenization
- Authorization and access control
- Key distribution
- Cloud component security
- Threat intelligence

The mechanisms are described as follows:

- *The definition and basic function* of the mechanism. The possible usages of the mechanism are mentioned as well in order to facilitate the application, e.g., symmetric encryption can be used for a storage encryption as well as for sending data to a client application with a session key.
- *The basic methods* used for the implementation of the mechanism, i.e., basic authorization methods, are manual PKE, ABE, and IBE.
- The *vulnerabilities* and *attacks* on a security mechanism.
- The *requirements* to the mechanism based on the attacks and vulnerabilities, e.g., authentication should use a strong password.

3.1 Authentication and Tokenization

3.1.1 Definition and Specific Characteristics

Before getting access to any protected information system, one should confirm his identity, in other words, authenticate himself. According to all international security standards [1, 2], authentication or managing the user identity is an obligatory

© The Author(s) 2016
T. Galibus et al., *Elements of Cloud Storage Security*, SpringerBriefs in
Computer Science, DOI 10.1007/978-3-319-44962-3_3

requirement for any protected computer system, i.e., there is no information security without the user identity management.

Definition Authentication is a procedure of confirming the identity of a user

The entrance point to the security system construction is one of the procedures that require special attention. According to many sources [3, 4] and authors' experience, authentication is a sensitive procedure that should be carefully selected and implemented. Authentication defines the way the identity of the user is verified and confirmed. In other words, authentication is a basis of a security framework. It specifies the characteristics of adversary and the possible attacks on a system as well.

In the cloud, the verification of user identity is even more important due to the nature of a cloud system, virtualization, and wider security perimeter [5–7].

The factors of importance:

1. Many recent company breaches are related to the authentication [4, 5].
2. The bring-your-own-device (BYOD) cloud environment can be accessed from any point and device. The proper management of user identities is the key to security.
3. The corporate cloud should provide the guarantee or the proof of user identity.

There is a practically single way to authenticate user: password + token/ PIN. Excessive requirements can be inconvenient for usability and efficiency. And vice versa the passwords are often compromised via social engineering and brute force attack.

Example 3.1 Dropbox.com authentication uses a user password and an automatically generated token. The security is the responsibility of a service user.

Example 3.2 Google.com moves toward the automatic login, i.e., the surveillance of various user-based factors is used to authenticate the user [8].

The corporate cloud security system begins with the secure authentication procedure. The authentication solution should never rely on an external provider. Authentication can be implemented as a service (SaaS), but the verification should be performed within the enterprise.

Therefore, the authentication service should not require more data than the password and PIN from the user and guarantee the security even when the client computer, portable device, or user password is compromised or stolen.

3.1.2 Types of Authentication

As mentioned above, the authentication setup cannot be performed by means of cryptographic services as cryptography cannot prove the identity of the key holder [9]. The authentication methods are heuristic, i.e., not provable. The

Fig. 3.1 Authentication security comparison

implementation of authentication mechanism depends on the resources or demands of a corporate cloud.

One-side authentication (*identity verification*) is the crucial part of any security architecture. The subdivisions of authentication are:

1. One factor/multifactor/strong (***Auth1/Auth2/Auth3***); this classification is based on the number of authentication factors to be verified and the diversity of the sources of information. The recent trend is to automatically verify the maximum possible number of user-based factors in order to verify the user identity [3, 9].
2. Direct/third party (***d/3p***), i.e., authentication can be implemented by the company itself or delegated to a third-party trusted authority via web interface, for example, using OpenID protocol [3, 10] or OAuth pseudo-authentication [11, 12].
3. Local/remote server (L/R), i.e., the user credentials can be verified on a local device or on a remote server via Kerberos [13]/LDAP [14] etc.
4. Recently emerging biometric authentication that can be verified directly and locally on a device [15, 16].
5. Endpoint authentication (EP) which additionally provides an interface for the device verification via the unsecured network.

From the point of security, the weakest form of authentication is the one-factor direct verification and the strongest one is three-factor (knowledge, possession and user identity) strong third-party authentication. Also, the local checkup of credential is weaker than the remote one if it is not the biometric authentication. Security of various authentication methods can be summarized in the flow represented in Fig. 3.1.

Additionally, the EP authentication can be part of Auth3/Auth2 protocol as the confirmation of the device validity.

The authentication method selection depends on many factors. Once the system functional and security requirements are defined, the authentication method can be configured. In other words, it depends on the confidentiality level and the core functionality of the corporate cloud. The corporate cloud storage always stores sensitive and important/confidential data, used for the private or corporate properties. This requires an authentication not weaker than *Auth2* (for the community and social services) and *Auth3* (extremely confidential governmental services). A smaller company may select to implement direct authentication, whereas a larger company should prefer to rely on a third-party authentication service. A weaker authentication in a distributed environment immediately leads to an obvious vulnerability. This analysis shows that there is a very strong connection between the type of authentication, the core functionality of the system, and the security demands.

Vulnerabilities Weak password, irresponsible user, one-factor authentication, and local authentication

Attacks Brute force attack, social engineering, attack on a device memory, and offline dictionary attack

Requirements

1. Guarantees the user identity and protection in the most common scenarios: the device is stolen, device is broken, and user password is compromised and misused.
2. Uses a strong password.
3. Is transparent.
4. Supports usability.

3.1.3   Usage of Tokens in the Cloud Storage

Authentication in the corporate cloud is to be performed on a remote server via LDAP3 [14], OAuth [11], or similar protocol. Tokenization [16] is a process of substituting the sensitive user data (login and password) with an access token generated from this data using a strong cryptographic algorithm, hash function with an appropriate cryptographic salt, or randomization [17]. Tokenization helps to secure the user-specific data when the device is compromised or stolen. The token can be based on the several components:

- User credentials: login and password
- User credentials and device ID or device key
- User credentials, device ID, and timestamp mark

In most cases, the strong hash functions like MD5 or randomization are the most effective methods to generate the token. The timestamp or Kerberos-based tokens [13] are not recommended because of the instability of synchronization between the server and device in the cloud environment.

The tokenization and de-tokenization processes can be implemented on a server, on a client, or on a third-party tokenization server. For the corporate environment, it is preferable to generate the token either on a server or in parallel on a client and server. The generated randomized value is used for the further communication between the server and the client [18–20] (Fig. 3.2).

Tokenization is performed before encryption and cryptographic key generation. The substituted value serves only for the simplified and secured user authentication procedure. The usage of token generated from a user login and password cannot substitute the two-factor authentication, as the token is generated automatically and is stored in the device memory. In other words, it allows the server to recognize the user-device pair.

The recent researches in security [21, 22] show that usage of tokenization procedure is often overestimated. That's why usage of the tokens should be protected by some additional user-backed data. It is recommended to use a constant or one-time PIN in order to support the tokenization in the BYOD environment:

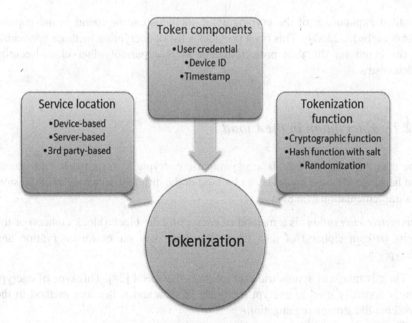

Fig. 3.2 Tokenization mechanism structure

1. The user is requested to enter a four-digit PIN every time the device is in idle for more than 5 min or after every share request or submission. This ensures that the user is still the one who entered the initial credentials. The adversary who tries to compromise or steal the device needs to perform the brute force attack on a PIN that can be prevented by the counting of the failed tries.
2. The user is requested to enter a one-time four-digit PIN sent to mobile device by SMS. The session should last longer than 5 min, similarly to the Internet banking session. This enhances the security and is, in fact, an implementation two-factor authentication. The device can be attacked, but the attack from different sources on a user account is prevented.

Attacks Man-in-the-middle, masquerade, brute force, and offline dictionary attacks

Vulnerabilities Sending token over insecure network without additional authentication support, using weak tokenization function

Requirements Strong function and additional support, i.e., PIN, user activity monitoring, or counting failed tries

3.2 Key Distribution and Data Encryption

This section explains the most widely used cryptographic techniques for the cloud storage protection. Using cryptographic services and methods relies on the key management methods including the key distribution, revocation, and storing.

Detailed explanation of the cryptographic methods can be found in the popular monographs [8, 23, 24]. This book provides a list of encryption methods applicable in the cloud for the data protection and as is a part of other cloud security mechanisms.

3.2.1 Encryption in the Cloud

The data encryption methods are symmetric encryption, asymmetric encryption, and hashing. All these methods can be used in the different scenarios of cloud storage implementation (see Sect. 4.8).

Symmetric encryption is a method of encrypting the block (block ciphers) or the digits (stream ciphers) of data where the same key serves for encryption and decryption.

The advantage of symmetric encryption is the speed [24]. This type of encryption is normally used to encrypt the bulks of data and is the core method in the protected file storage organization.

The disadvantage is the necessity to send the key over the insecure network, which requires a specific key distribution method to be implemented (see Sect. 3.2.3).

The industry currently uses the following methods of symmetric encryption:

- AES [25] is a block cipher that became an international standard and uses the blocks of 128, 192, and 256 bits. The throughput on the modern processors is up to 700 Mb/s [26].
- Twofish [23] is the block cipher and the competing algorithm with AES. The block length is 128, 192, and 256 bits. On most platforms it is slower than AES, but there have been developed less attacks on this cipher so far.
- RC4 [8, 23] is the popular stream cipher implemented in many cryptographic APIs. It is fast, convenient, but very insecure [27].

Symmetric encryption is normally used in the following security components:

- Protected storage encryption
- Client data at rest encryption
- Protecting the temporarily confidential data
- Mutual authentication via Kerberos [13]

Vulnerabilities One shared key, wide range of attacks and cryptanalysis methods [28, 29], necessity to renovate the key

Attacks

1. Necessity to send the key over insecure network (MITM attack) [21]
2. Masquerade attack
3. A practically reasonable time for cryptanalysis [28]

The requirements to the block cipher implementation:

1. Support the key renewal mechanism.
2. Keep the keys to the encrypted data in a protected storage.
3. Use secured key generation mechanism.
4. Utilize the protected distribution mechanism.

Asymmetric encryption or public-key encryption (PKE) is encryption that uses the pairs of keys: public key that is distributed in the clear is paired with a private key known only to the owner. PKE has two basic functions. It can be used to authenticate the private key owner or to ensure that only private key owner can decrypt the message. The security of PKE relies on the computational complexity of certain mathematical problems, i.e., discrete logarithm computation or elliptic curve relationships. The private key does not need to be distributed in order to ensure the message privacy. Thus, generally PKE is considered more secure than symmetric encryption. But due to the computational complexity, asymmetric encryption can be used for sending only the small portions of confidential data, i.e., session keys. Session key is usually a symmetric encryption key that serves for encryption and decryption of the whole file share. The common methods of PKE are:

1. RSA [30]: most wide-spread PKE standard, but the key length (2,048 bits minimum) and the computational complexity make it less appealing for the cloud-based systems.
2. ECDSA [31]: a current PKE standard in many countries. It provides the same level of security with a key length and computational complexity much less than RSA (256 bit key security is equal to security of 3,072 bit RSA [32]).
3. PBC [33]: mostly used for the attribute-based and identity-based encryption (see Sect. 3.3). As a consequence, it requires careful implementation and longer period for deployment due to the lack of trusted PBC methods in the common cryptography libraries.

The functions of PKE in the protected cloud storage are numerous:

1. Session key or share key encryption
2. Authentication of the private key owner
3. Encrypted key exchange [34] for the protected key distribution (see Sect. 3.2.3)
4. Attribute-based encryption [33] for the fine-grained access control support
5. Mutual authentication to assure the identity of both client and server in order to avoid man-in-the-middle attacks

Attacks and vulnerabilities

1. Masquerade [23]: substituting all messages between the owner of the private key and the sender can be performed if no trusted authority is used in communication.
2. MITC attack [21] can be achieved for special types of PKE such as ABE where distributing private key cannot be avoided.
3. Side channel attack [35, 36].
4. Attack on an endpoint device protected memory.

Requirements for PKE implementation

1. The cloud environment requires the implementation of key revocation and key renovation methods. With regard to these functions, PKE key generation procedure should be computationally efficient. That's why it's important to select a reasonably secure and fast PKE algorithm.
2. The key generation must be implemented with secure pseudorandom number generator.
3. The key length and other parameters should provide sufficient encryption and decryption procedures on execution time and reasonable security [23].

Hashing [23] is an encryption without a key, i.e., encryption based on a cryptographic hash or one-way function. Such function is infeasible to invert and maps data of arbitrary size to a string of fixed size.

The common methods of hashing are MD5, SHA-1, SHA-2, and SHA-3. MD5 and SHA-1 are no longer considered secure, and SHA-3 is advanced SHA-2 version [37]. The functions of hashing are:

1. Transferring the authentication data securely, namely, login and password
2. Generating the digital signature
3. Storing the PIN code verification data
4. Token generation

Attacks

1. The hashed portion can be used for the masquerade attack if it is not enhanced with a timestamp.
2. Offline dictionary attack on a stolen hashed value is always possible.

Requirements

1. Use hash along with the timestamp or a stronger algorithm.
2. Hash function should be fast.
3. Implementation should be protected.

3.2.2 Additional Methods

Secret Sharing [38, 39] aims to secure the functions of sharing and combining the confidential information among the trusted participants. The confidential value or the secret key is distributed among the group of participants so that only authorized subgroups can restore the original secret by pooling their shares together. At the same time, it guarantees that getting any number of shares does not give any information of the secret if they are not authorized.

It is recommended to use Shamir secret sharing [38] for small groups of participants and modular secret sharing based on polynomials [39] as soon as the number of participants exceeds 20 due to the efficiency considerations.

SS can be implemented in the cloud storage in order to enhance the security of key storing and distributing. The protected master-key value is split between several trusted authorities in a secure manner so that even if one of the authorities is compromised the master key is not affected. The authorities agree on the combined key restoring procedure.

The usage of (n, n)-threshold SS guarantees that only possession of all parts of the secret allows to restore the shared value correctly. Otherwise, the adversary is able to reconstruct the randomly generated value.

Trusted Timestamping [40, 41] is a cryptographic service providing a secured time record in order to verify the modification or creation time of certain message. The trusted timestamping mechanisms can provide generation of independent tokens or linked tokens. The independent tokens are produced by means of PKE or MAC signature. The linked tokens are produced by a linear hash value chain or Merkle tree, i.e., binary hash tree.

Using timestamp is crucial for key distribution and key revocation as it guarantees the security from the masquerade attack and solves as a proof of key validity.

3.2.3   Key Distribution

In the cloud environment, the problem of key distribution requires special attention due to the agents' transparency [42]. Commonly, key distribution methods [8] are based on PKE and Diffie-Hellman protocol symmetric encryption (tokenization [18] or Kerberos protocol [13]). More sophisticated methods with higher security level are EKE- [34] and SS-based schemes similar to [43] (Table 3.1).

The corporate cloud storage requires the key distribution algorithm setup as the keys are to be transferred to users by the trusted centralized authority. Key distribution must be protected with a stronger algorithm than the following protected data.

The attacks on key distribution module are based on the underlying encryption methods:

1. MITM: Adversary steals the value of the session key and uses it for cryptanalysis or masquerade.
2. Inserting the wrong data into the communication flow.
3. Side channel attacks.

3.2.4   Key Storing and Using

The keys are usually guarded in a specific protected storage. The master key protects key storage on a server or client. This key storage must follow the general key management requirements [32]. The main requirements are:

Table 3.1 Key distribution mechanisms

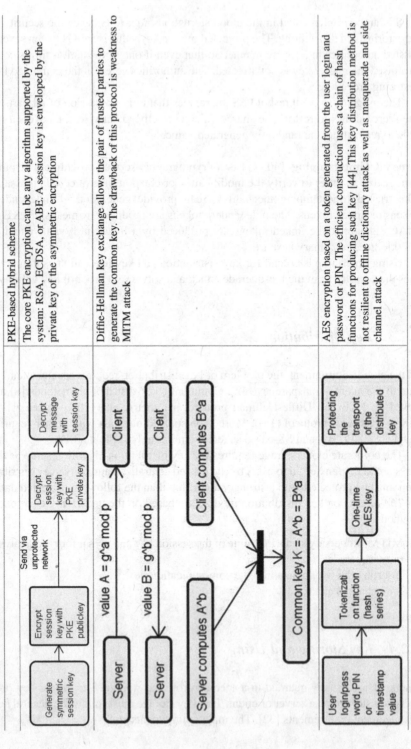

PKE-based hybrid scheme

The core PKE encryption can be any algorithm supported by the system: RSA, ECDSA, or ABE. A session key is enveloped by the private key of the asymmetric encryption

Diffie-Hellman key exchange allows the pair of trusted parties to generate the common key. The drawback of this protocol is weakness to MITM attack

AES encryption based on a token generated from the user login and password or PIN. The efficient construction uses a chain of hash functions for producing such key [44]. This key distribution method is not resilient to offline dictionary attack as well as masquerade and side channel attack

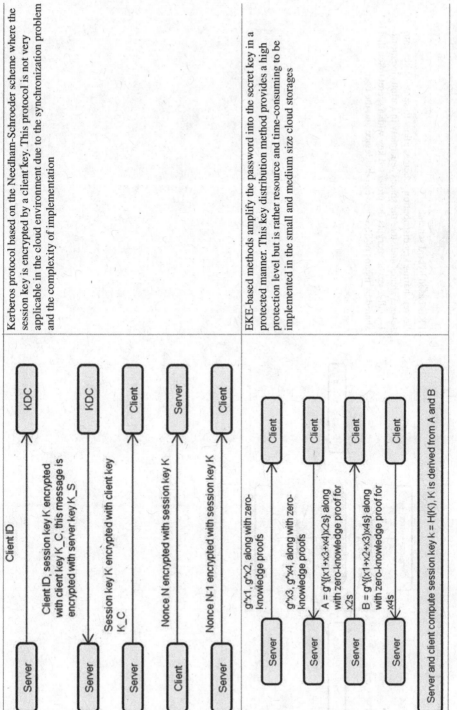

Kerberos protocol based on the Needham-Schroeder scheme where the session key is encrypted by a client key. This protocol is not very applicable in the cloud environment due to the synchronization problem and the complexity of implementation

EKE-based methods amplify the password into the secret key in a protected manner. This key distribution method provides a high protection level but is rather resource and time-consuming to be implemented in the small and medium size cloud storages

(continued)

Table 3.1 (continued)

PKE-based hybrid scheme
Secret sharing key distribution schemes allow to split the key into several shares and store the shares separately in various locations. Usually, server encrypts the protected key with a secret token that is shared by means of SSS between the device and the user

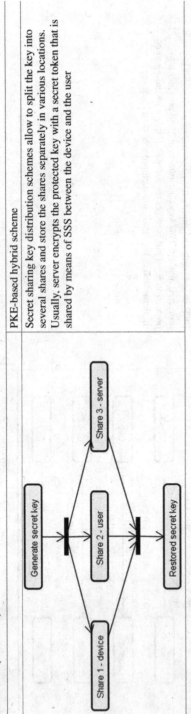

1. A separate key storage, i.e., the encrypted data, is stored in another memory location.
2. Master key is generated in a secure way.
3. Key storage supports either key renovation method, i.e., master key expires or uses a strong PKE.
4. Use additional methods like distributed master-key storing via SSS to enhance protection.
5. The keys should be deleted from unprotected memory after usage.

3.3 Authorization and Access Control Support

3.3.1 Definition and Implementation of Access Control

Once the user identity is specified, the system should be able to authorize the user to access the data portions. The protected storage data is accessed only by the permitted users, according to the security model and policies. The access policies are based on the user attributes [45] and include his role in organization, security parameter specification, etc. The authorization authority in the corporate cloud is centralized, i.e., the server decides the user access rights and generates the keys.

Authorization is a part of access control procedure, which is divided into two phases:

1. Definition of access policies
2. Application of access policies, i.e., granting access

Authorization function is applied on the first phase of AC procedure. Authorization is the mechanism which allows to set up the various access policies, i.e., generate and distribute the keys according to user access rights and policies.

Definition Authorization is a function/mechanism of specifying access rights or access policy

The step-by-step authorization implementation is shown in Fig. 3.3.

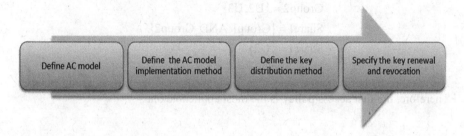

Fig. 3.3 Authorization implementation

3.3.2 Access Control Models and Policies

User access rights are specified through the AC models based on various access criteria, i.e., attributes, roles, hierarchy etc. [46]. In the corporate cloud environment, it is recommended to follow one of the basic access scenarios. In the cloud storage, the protected shares, i.e., groups of files, can be accessed by the authorized groups of users. Generally, this policy follows the ABAC model [45]. The particular authorization schemes within ABAC model are as follows:

- Simple group access policy
  The set of user groups authorized to access specific share is specified directly:

$$Group1 = \{U1, U2\}$$
$$Share1 = \{Group1\}$$
$$Group1 = \{Share1\}$$

- Hierarchy of user groups
  The access rules can follow a hierarchy policy. In this case, if a group is authorized to specific share, any group that contains it is automatically authorized to the same share:

$$Group1 = \{U1, U2\}$$
$$Group2 = \{U3, U4\}$$
$$Group3 = \{Group1, Group2\}$$
$$Share1 = \{Group3\} \text{ then } Share1 = \{U1, U2, U3, U4\}$$

- Complex group attribute policy
  Sometimes it is necessary to organize access policy that contains the specific access rules, i.e., one share can be accessible to users that belong to Group1 AND Group2.

$$Group1 = \{U1, U2\}$$
$$Group2 = \{U2, U3\}$$
$$Share1 = \{Group1 \text{ AND } Group2\}$$
$$Share1 = \{U2\}$$

All specific authorization policies can be implemented by simple group policy. Therefore, the first access policy is the most applicable one.

3.3.3 Access Control Methods

Authorization is specified by access rules, encryption method and the key distribution mechanism. Authorization includes the definition of user identity; therefore, it is preceded by authentication in the security system configuration.

The basic methods of user authorization are:

1. PKE-based manual attribute generation

   - The user attributes, i.e., randomly generated values, are stored on a server. Each attribute matches to a group of users.
   - The groups can be authorized to access file shares as specified by the correspondence tables on a server.
   - Each attribute is matched by a private key of PKE. The private keys are generated on server and sent to users via protected channel (see Sect. 3.2.3).
   - The public keys of PKE are stored on a server and are matched by the attributes, i.e., groups.
   - Each time an authorized user wishes to access the share, he sends a request signed by his private key. The server searches the corresponding attribute set specified by used ID and finds the corresponding public key, and if it is valid, the share is sent to the user.
   - The disadvantage of this method is the necessity to setup the attributes ad their correspondence manually. Such method is applicable only for the small corporate cloud storages where the amount of authorization data is easily processed manually. Key revocation and renovation are difficult to achieve.

2. Identity-based encryption

   - Identity-based encryption (IBE) [47, 48] allows to control the public-key generation based on the user credentials, i.e., user ID. In other words, it doesn't require the distribution of the public keys and keeping the matching tables on a server as the public keys corresponding to the attributes are derived from the master public key and user ID. The drawback of this approach is the absence of key revocation and the necessity to store the user attribute matching tables. The security of the system relies on the security of private key generator (PKG) and the protected channel between the client and the PKG.

3. Attribute-based encryption

   - Attribute-based access control [33] is a most perspective cryptographic method for the authorization support. ABE directly links the user attributes to a user private key, i.e., there is no need to store a matching table. The keys of the encryption are generated automatically in order to match the user access rights. Unfortunately, this perspective AC mechanism is not widely implemented in the cloud environment due to the complexity of core cryptography methods. It was implemented in the Storgrid [49] protected cloud storage with the following additional parameters to support the flexible attribute generation and revocation.

Solution 3.1: Protocol ABE-STR [3.50]
Master key (MK) is kept safely on server and accessible only for the domain administrator:

$$MK = (t_1, \ldots, t_n, y)$$

The values t_i are randomly selected from the huge group Z_p. They are the private keys corresponding to the group attributes.

Public key (PK) depends on the master-key values and is kept in the clear allowing users to access the information:

$$PK = \left(g^{t_1}, \ldots, g^{t_n}, Y = e(g,g)^y \right)$$

Here $e(g,g)$ is the bilinear pairing.

User KEY_SET depends on his attribute set. Here each D_i (GROUP_SHARE_KEY) serves for decryption of the data of a single share of a single group of users:

$$\{t_i\}_U \rightarrow D = \left\{ D_i = g^{yw/t_i} \right\}$$

Encryption of the text M, i.e., FILE_KEY, or the permanent AES symmetric key is multiplication. The set of the public keys E_i (PUBLIC_SHARE_KEY) corresponding to the specific group able to access the specific share is kept along with the encrypted text:

$$E = Me(g,g)^{ys}, \left\{ E_i = g^{t_i s/w} \right\}_{\forall i \in \{t_i\} M}$$

Decryption is division:

$$M = E / Y^s$$

In order to perform this operation, the user needs D_i corresponding to the secret attribute t_i and

$$Y^s = e(g,g)^{ys} = e(E_i, D_i) = e\left(g^{\frac{yw}{t_i}}, g^{t_i s/w} \right) = e(g,g)^{ys}$$

3.3.4 Key Renewal and Revocation

Important requirement in the protected cloud environment is the necessity to support the rapid and periodical key renewal/revocation. The key expiry period is one of the most efficient methods to provide the sufficient security level to the cloud storage. At the same time, the usability of the system should not be affected. The modified ABE access control method [50] allows to support the automatic key renewal and revocation based on the key parameter regeneration.

> **Solution 3.2: Key Revocation Protocol ABE-STR**
> User U is deleted from the group $Group_i$. Server asks for the group attribute t_i.
>   Server modifies the parameter w for the group $Group_i$.
>   Server modifies private authorization key for the group $Group_i$ D_i.
>   Server uses this value to communicate to all group members using some secure key distribution method.
>   Server modifies the public keys E_{ij} for each share j in $Group_i$. Server sends this value to the group members in the clear. The group members do not need to re-download the files.
>   The expired public share authorization keys corresponding to the $Group_i$ are deleted from the revoked device. User cannot get access anymore to the K_F (the file share key).

3.3.5 Authorization Vulnerabilities, Attacks, and Requirements

Access control is one of the most difficult tasks in the cloud environment. While configuring the authorization in the cloud, it is recommended:

1. The common attacks depend on the core encryption and key distribution method applied. Due to the key expiry period and the necessity to support the key revocation, there is a high possibility of MITC/MITM attack [21]. Therefore, it is necessary to implement the user activities monitoring along with the protected encryption implementation and key transport.
2. The core of ABE is PBC [33], which is rarely implemented in the well-tested and optimized cryptographic libraries. Therefore, the deployment and testing of the ABE-based authorization is a longer procedure compared to other methods.
3. It is highly recommended to implement the key revocation/renewal or at least the user activities monitoring in order to avoid the highly confidential data compromised due to the information leakage related to the old key misuse.

3.4   Threat Intelligence

Cloud environments and Internet of things are examples of new technologies available using the Internet. Both contributed to the creation of new business models and activities and broad communications capacities using mobile technologies. But on the other hand, such technologies increase significantly the surface for attacks. There are real cyber threats, anonymity solutions, attacks to financial systems, information theft, and many more activities that undermine the security to such solutions and technologies.

Over the past of the last 10 years, these threats have become much more sophisticated. The attackers' capabilities and the ability of innovating new techniques are faster than the protection solutions can accomplish. In this sense, many solutions applied to detect and combat cyber threats were developed and succeeded for a short period of time. For example, the intrusion detection systems (IDS), intrusion prevention systems (IPS), and security information and event management (SIEM) are widely known solutions in the information security markets.

Based on the increasing need to deal with cyber threats in the information security area, experts bothered to develop mechanisms and tools for detection and protection of computer systems. Much of this effort is by the use of technologies such as predictive data analysis, behavioral monitoring, artificial intelligence, devices behavior, protocols analysis, and many other resources in informational systems, computer networks, and information security fields.

In other words, the knowledge required to deal with cyber threats requires contextualization, means and indicators, direct and indirect implications, warnings, monitoring new threats to assets, and critical infrastructure systems. All this is used together to support strategic decisions and measures that may be applied in each situation.

As result of such, advances in the use of such technologies comes the threat intelligence definition.

Threat intelligence is able to provide the ability to recognize and act quickly in attack scenarios. This is possible through the consolidation of internal data sources, information sharing throughout reliable partners and specialized institutions in information security, and also support by private and public sectors, which can build reputation systems.

A general definition of threat intelligence is the evidence-based knowledge, which includes context, means, guides, inferences, and/or actionable advice, in order to mitigate or protect about an existing or emerging threat to assets. This knowledge can be used to support decisions regarding the response actions to stop or avoid that threat to cyber environments and information systems.

Dealing with such problems is impossible without humans, because they require deep knowledge in information security and communications, information assets, auditing, engineering, and others that might be necessary.

But of course, the amount of information to be analyzed also needs computer systems and information security solutions because to be able to monitor and follow

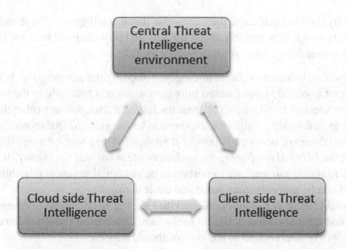

Fig. 3.4 The threat intelligence usage scenario

cyber threats, some process cannot be achieved without being automated. The amount of data is such that it is impossible for humans to process it without information systems, security systems, correlational systems, big data analytics, etc. But on the other hand, all these systems cannot be fully automated with current technology available.

Threat intelligence applied to cloud systems should consider basically two perspectives. The first perspective is the client side (be it a desktop or mobile solution), which consumes services offered but also generates enormous amount of information. The second perspective is the cloud provider side, which is responsible for guaranties regarding level of services and availability of its services. Cloud providers also need to deliver security to the clients. A central environment controls these two perspectives. Figure 3.4 illustrates this scenario.

On the client side, there are applications developed to easy access to cloud infrastructure, such as mobile applications, browsers, plug-ins, full client-side applications that need to be installed on the costumer side, and even other solutions that can be used to secure the environment of the client.

Regarding the cloud provider side, data about threats, attacks, and behavior can be processed on the cloud side environment and sent to the central threat intelligence so it can be analyzed using advanced technologies.

The client side may be able to analyze user behavior and application specific usage and collect data to be processed and also to be correlated to other indicators on the cloud side and central threat intelligence.

All these perspectives are briefly detailed below.

Central Threat Intelligence Environment

The central threat intelligence is responsible to correlate all of the gathered information by using diverse algorithms and data-mining techniques. This part of the solution is responsible to store, process, and give visibility to various types of information provided by the cloud side and the client-side threat intelligence. These techniques will identify suspicious patterns and behaviors and provide great help for intrusion detection and auditing. Most of its activities include:

1. Data mining solutions – threat intelligence should take advantage of being able to extract knowledge from stored information already available to the system in order to identify trends, new patterns, unclassified data, and any other thing that can help isolate what might be uncommon to the system. Questions like *What was the abnormal activity? When did it happen? Where was it found? What does it look like? How is it affecting the environment? What was the impact? What was the surrounding context?* are important to be answered as fast as possible so new threats can be properly discovered and dealt with.
2. Artificial intelligence – abnormal activities should be addressed to AI engines to learn fast what abnormal activities looks like. Thus, it can generate alerts to situations where intervention to the system should happen.
3. Correlate behavioral analysis – being able to address user activities to previous data collected can produce a confidence rating on whether the user activity is authentic or not. This kind of capabilities can be applied in both user environment and network environment. In such cases, the use of algorithms to determine whether a threat to the system is being actively deployed is important to take decisions before an attack can cause significant damage.
4. Predictive analysis – this should apply statistical models to data collected from cloud environment and client environment to identify what kind of data are likely malicious and could be used to predict future attacks.

Knowledge generated from the central threat intelligence can be distributed to both cloud threat intelligence and client sides. This way threats can be stopped efficiently than using static signatures.

Cloud Side Requirements
The cloud provider must have the ability to check data in and out of its infrastructure to search for known threats such as malware that can destroy or corrupt user data. In the case of unknown threats, the use of the same kind of technologies applied to central threat intelligence can be deployed restricting its horizon just to the services provided by the cloud itself.

Basically this infrastructure needs to collect, analyze, and process data from multiple sources such as:

1. Servers logs – this is important because many activities that actually happened are based on the values contained in logs file. This gives indicators about when, how, and by whom a server is used. Basically using logs files gives the cloud provider the ability to generate various information on demand and also to extract indicators of compromise of a system, i.e., an entry in the log, which indicates a user had access to a file it was not supposed to.
2. Middleware and middleware components data – most cloud solutions use middleware components to exchange information from multiple information sys-

tems. This information can provide indicators of the use of computer resources, the amount of information exchanged, to whom that information was processed for, or the amount of messages related to a particular module of the system. Such information is important to the cloud provider to check if the system is working properly or some resources are being overloaded with requests where it should not.

3. Network flows – detailing how packet information flows from one point to another gives the visibility to security analysts of how the information flows in the systems and what are the entities responsible for such flow. It also gives indicators of how many times that happened, when that happened, if the connections were normal or ended abruptly, the amount of information exchanged, the mean values of connections, etc.

4. Storage data – this is important because it gives administrators information detailing how the behavior of file I/O is, the file system usage like slow reads, slow writes, too many reads for one file, too many copies of one single file, recursively reading and writing, and other indicators.

5. Virtual network devices information – this is important to verify how the virtual devices are being used and which of them could be overloaded, which one is not being used at all, the amount of information generated by particular devices, and any other indicators that can be of use.

Client-Side Requirements

The client application must have the ability to check what is happening in its user level domain. It needs to be able to perform some data analyses by itself and send detailed information of what is happening in its environment both to cloud threat intelligence and central intelligence.

Commonly, client applications use most indicators like geolocation of the device to trace its usage, setting up the expiration period of an app, secured transfer politics between apps, restricting access to the corporate app, setting up the expiration period of app pass/pin, setting up the counter of failed tries, restricted or prohibited offline access, and basic logging and auditing.

Besides the most commonly used indicators, the client-side infrastructure needs to collect, analyze, and process data such as:

1. Cloud usage – the application can provided client-side information and indicators that show how much information the user is consuming or demanding from the cloud provider. The app cloud also checks the health of the cloud services the user is using and the amount of the traffic generated in a communication process.

2. User behavior – the client-side application could have software module responsible to check and verify what are the actions performed by the user, which frequency do they happen, how many files the user has, what are the particularities of the files (file attributes), and how many times a particular file is requested, so caching techniques can be deployed delivering faster information. The most important is to address if this behavior can be classified as normal or abnormal in the perspective of what the user used to do.

3. App behavior – the client side may use particular controls that check if the normal operations performed by the applications, such as data sent and received from the cloud provider, are to be considered normal. Also the application itself can take security measures which needs attention by the cloud provider, for example, blocking unauthenticated users, or if the application is generating errors and what type of errors they are, if the application is being used by other processes of the operational system differently of the normal ones, and many other indicators which are to be considered important.
4. Local log analysis – the application must generate some log information, and the application must be able to analyze it in terms of common usage statistics, normal operations, abnormal behavior, and other indicators instead of just sending the log to processing.

Another important information that can be applied to threat intelligence capabilities is to enumerate in order of importance what kind of technology can be applied in each case and how much resources it needs to operate.

Considering the client side, for instance, let us assume the client application should have three different threat intelligence mechanisms – log analysis, app behavior, and user behavior.

Now, the question is what are the levels of importance and priority a modulus should have based on the type of information it needs to perform threat intelligence?

Depending on the type of cloud provider, one may consider more important functions about log analysis processing in the client side then checking the health of the application itself. Thus, log analysis should have higher priority in terms of use in the client side.

Of course this kind of classification depends on subjective evaluations by the cloud provider itself. Decisions about what kind of data should be sent to threat intelligence processing are more important when compared to other types of data that should be properly defined first. With such decisions addressed appropriately, the cloud provider can build knowledge to help address security problems in the cloud solutions.

3.5   Cloud Storage Component Security

In this section, the basic concepts and mechanisms applicable for the cloud storage components are described.

The components of the cloud storage as it is mentioned in Chap. 2 are server, client, and mobile device. The server is considered the most protected cloud component, while the mobile device is considered the least protected component and the source of data leakage. The biggest amount of protected data is stored on a server, while the smaller portions can be preserved on a client or mobile device. The security of the cloud storage is centered on the protection of data storing and transferring.

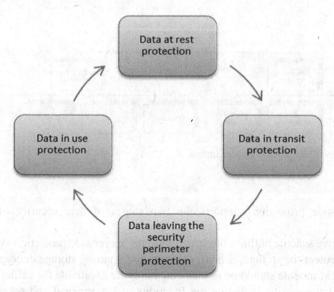

Fig. 3.5 Component security chart

The data security subsystems serve for the data protection at each phase of the cloud storage life cycle:

1. *Protecting data at rest/at the endpoint* includes the mechanisms that assure the security of data stored on a server or a client device.
2. *Protecting data in transit* includes the mechanisms and protocols for the security of the data transportation in the cloud environment.
3. *Protecting data in use* includes the procedure of protected viewing, modifying, and syncing data on a client and mobile device along server.
4. *Protecting the data that leaves the security perimeter* includes an offline mode protection for the mobile device and protection of the data that leaves the security perimeter.

The methods and mechanisms of the previous sections are used in order to formulate the security concept in all phases of data processing and storing life cycle in the cloud storage (Fig. 3.5).

3.5.1 Server-Side Protection

The server is not used for the protected data usage but rather to provide the efficient and reliable data storing. That's why the strongest security mechanisms on a server serve for data at rest. Also, server supports the data syncing and is responsible for data in transit protection in the communication with the client (the server verifies the client credentials as a trusted authority).

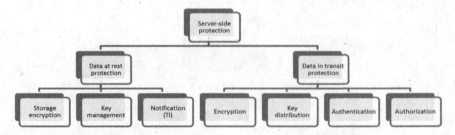

Fig. 3.6 Server-side protection mechanisms

Server-side protection supports the two stages of data security life cycle (Fig. 3.6).

The above scheme outlines the structure of the server-side protection system. In order to protect the storage, it is necessary to use a strong storage encryption. An efficient KM module should be implemented in order to provide the sufficient level of master-key security, including the functions of key renewal and regeneration. The notifications of the threat intelligence unit help administrator to keep control of the synchronization activities.

Server is responsible for securing the data transport and for managing the user identities. That's why the core key generation and encryption methods for the authentication, authorization, and key distribution mechanisms are to be implemented on a server.

Due to the specific security requirements and the availability of resources, it is highly recommended to implement the re-encryption mechanism of the server storage (see Chap. 4).

The main features of the server-side protection are:

1. Strong encryption method for data at rest (no resource limitation)
2. Implementation of all key generation and distribution procedures
3. Constant enhanced TI monitoring

Vulnerabilities Synchronization of corrupted files, weak password or token, weak distribution method, re-encryption, and weak master-key and weak key storage protection

Attacks Ransomware attack, MITC attack on user token and user password, virus attack, attack during re-encryption, and attack on a master-key or key storage

Requirements are:

1. Server should use a proper key protection method, i.e., corresponding to the type of a cloud and the confidentiality level.
2. Encryption should be secure but should not slow down the data procession.
3. The extensive reporting should be implemented.

4. A specific ransomware checkup should be performed before sending or submitting the user files.

In Chap. 4, the efficient server-side protection schemes are proposed in connection with different types of cloud storages.

3.5.2 Client-Side Protection

Despite the cloud service models, IaaS, PaaS, or SaaS, the client-side protection is a concern that has to be taken into account while using cloud-based services. Notice that the responsibility for the protection in the client side is not the same for the three models, i.e., depending on the service model, the cloud provider has more responsibility in relation to the security issue. The cloud provider has a given responsibility for IaaS provision, which is augmented for the PaaS model, and achieves its highest level in the SaaS model. However in all cases the user accesses the data via a network channel that can be the Internet, which represents a non-controlled zone by which the data traffic flows, i.e., this concerns the data in transit and data in use. Thus, it is possible to organize the client-side protection according to two classes: data security and channel security, as depicted in Fig. 3.7. Channel security aspects are related to network security measures and interface security, which will be further detailed in Sect. 3.5.4.

Data Security
The data security aspect concerns about the data confidentiality, availability, and integrity, affecting both data at rest and data in transit. The following subcategories can be listed:

1. Cryptography: *Different parts of the data need to be encrypted, not only in the server but also in the client side. Different types of cryptography techniques can be used, depending on the client devices and the SLAs agreed between the cloud provider and the client, as well as legal aspects, for instance, compliance with rules such as Sarbanes-Oxley Act.*
2. Redundancy: *Despite being a major concern in the server side, it is also important that redundancy of information not yet sent from the client to the cloud, i.e., data in use, be assured. Temporary buffers represent a possible way to surpass this problem.*

Fig. 3.7 Client-side
protection dimensions

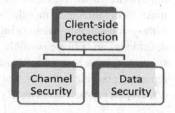

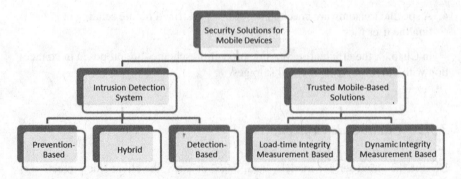

Fig. 3.8 Classification of the most prominent security solutions for mobile devices

3. Discard of temporary data: *Related to the above redundancy is the discard of temporary data. Depending on the way temporary files are stored in the client side, they may allow recovery of sensitive data that should not be in the client side after uploaded to the cloud, for instance, when file systems such as Ext3, which only removes the index entries from the data allocation tables, are used.*

3.5.3 Mobile Device Protection

Despite the client-side protection discussed above, considering mobile devices accessing the cloud, additional care must be considered in relation to security. One of important aspects to be taken into account in relation to mobile device protection is the fact that they can leave the physical limits of the company. So besides the concerns about data at rest, data in transit, and data in use, it is also important to take care about the data leaving the premises. In order to cope with the challenges posed by the mobile devices protection, security mechanisms have to be adapted to their environment and modes of operation. These mechanisms can be of different types, but it is possible to concentrate a number of them as intrusion detection systems for smartphones and as trusted mobile-based solutions [51], as can be seen in Fig. 3.8.

The first class can act both in the prevention, by using digital signatures, for instance, or in the effective detection and identification of a malicious activity. The particular security solutions vary much, depending on the detection principle, the collected data to perform the detection, the architectural type, and the target operating system. However, interesting similarities among them can be observed, which make them suitable to mobile devices. One common aspect that is explored is the battery consumption monitoring. Depending on the normal consumption profile, deviations can indicate possible malicious activities. Sandboxing is also a common solution approach, in which hardware modules that are not frequently used and that represent possible breaches that can be explored by malicious software are turned off. Thus, it is possible to classify them in two groups according to the used approach:

1. Prevention-based approach: *Solutions based on this approach use digital signatures, cryptography algorithms, and hash functions. They are able to assure properties like confidentiality, authentication, and integrity of data at rest and in transit.*
2. Detection-based approach: *Solutions based on the detection approach work as mechanisms to identify attacks, which can affect data in use, in transit, or leaving the premises. They can use an anomaly-based strategy, in which they compare the normal behavior with the observed one applying machine learning and power consumption monitoring, or a signature-based strategy, in which a base of patterns of well-known attacks is used to identify the occurrence of an attack. These patterns can be manually or automatically defined, depending on how the base of attacks is built.*
3. Hybrid approach: *Solutions exploring mechanisms of both approaches mentioned above are classified as hybrid solutions. They try to get benefit of the advantages of each one in an attempt to minimize their drawbacks. For example, a detection-based solution may explore both a signature-based strategy, which would not recognize abnormal behaviors, and an anomaly-based strategy, so that any behavior deviation could be considered as a possible threat to be further investigated. Another possible combination could be the use of a prevention-based strategy using hash functions to assess the integrity of downloaded software and the continued monitoring of its behavior using an anomaly detection strategy.*

The second class, the trusted mobile, is based on different ways to attest the software and hardware integrity. The solutions vary from hashing, asymmetric encryption, generation, and verification of signatures as well as the use of third trusted parties. Cryptography primitives can be used to implement hardware-based security services, such as integrity measurement, authentication, or secure boot [52]. A common explored idea here is the usage of a third trusted party to attest the integrity of value that is used to verify a given piece of software code or accessed data. The solutions for integrity measurement in this second class can be classified as load-time or dynamic measurements, as follows:

- *Load-time integrity measurement-based solutions*: These solutions are applied both to software code and data in use or leaving the premises. Pieces of code or data are measured when they are loaded into the volatile main memory. This integrity verification is done before the software is executed or the data is used.
- *Dynamic integrity measurement-based solutions*: These solutions target the software of critical applications when they are executing, i.e., at run-time, thus directly affecting data in use.

Additionally, the mobile devices should support the offline security infrastructure, i.e., they have to provide a strategy of protecting the data once they go offline. In order to accomplish this goal, they use the following operations:

1. Protected storage operations – This first group of operations includes requesting the user to enter with the PIN code upon performing a storage operation, com-

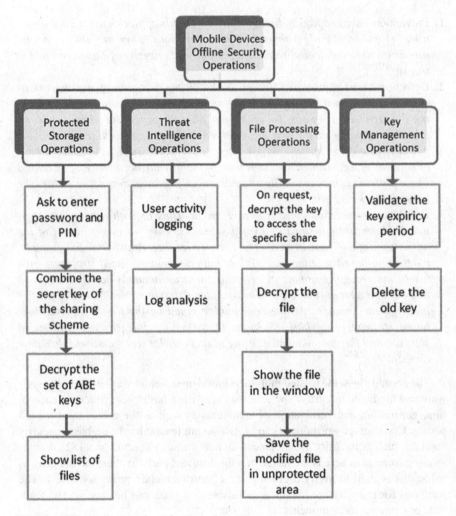

Fig. 3.9 Offline mode operations chart

bining the secret key of the shared scheme, decrypting the set of ABE keys, and showing the list of files.

2. Threat intelligence operations – This second group of operations includes logging the user's activities and analyzing the logs.
3. File processing operations – This third group of operations includes decrypting the key to access a specific share upon request, decrypting the requested file, showing the file, and saving the modifications of the file in an unprotected area.
4. Key management operations – This last group includes validating the key expiry period and deleting the old key.

Figure 3.9 summarizes the offline security protection operations.

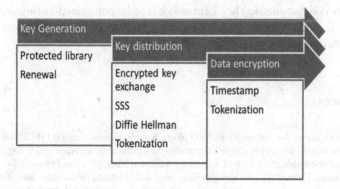

Fig. 3.10 Channel security scheme

3.5.4   Channel Protection Mechanisms

The channels in the protected cloud storage serve for syncing the server and client data. Users have limited modification capabilities so the traffic from the server to client is more intense. Additionally, server is considered a trusted authority (a corporate organization center) and the mutual authentication is not necessary. The server authenticates and authorizes the clients and portable devices.

The data transfer channel protection in the distributed environment relies on cryptographic methods, i.e., the data encryption and key distribution methods (see Sect. 3.2). The data in transit protection depends on the configuration of KM and DE modules. The structural channel security scheme is presented in Fig. 3.10.

As it is stated in Sect. 1.4 in the protected corporate environment, the control over the data privacy is not the responsibility of a particular user. Server generates and manages the keys and maintains the access control. That's why server manages the cryptographic procedures and protocols in order to protect the key transit and the data transit to a client or a portable device.

In a corporate environment, the channel security scheme should use all these three essential steps as a user does not get a complete control over his keys. That's why in the practical scenarios, ABE along with key distribution are used in place of PKE.

Besides the cryptography-based security aspects, as previously stated in Sect. 3.3.2, channel security depends on the network security. The following additional measures are related to network security:

- *Data in transit*: In order to mitigate vulnerabilities related to the data communication network in which this data flows, an advisable security measure is the usage of virtual private networks (VPN) to assure protection from network vulnerabilities.
- *Firewalling*: Besides the security that firewalls can provide to the cloud provider, it is important that cloud clients use firewall, so that they can protect the end of the cloud architecture against attacks such as denial of service, phishing, among many others.

- *Security configurations*: The client side has to be configured having security in mind. This means that security aware measures such as software updates have to be regularly applied.

References

1. Common Criteria for Information Technology Security Evaluation ISO\IEC 15408 (2005) Common criteria portal. http://www.commoncriteriaportal.org/cc/. Accessed 6 July 2016
2. NIST Special Publication 800-14 Generally Accepted Principles and Practices for Securing Information Technology Systems (1996) National Institute Standards and Technology Computer Security Division. http://csrc.nist.gov/publications/PubsSPs.html. Accessed 6 July 2016
3. Lopez M (2013) 4 reasons why you need stronger authentication now. Symantec Official Blog. http://www.symantec.com/connect/blogs/4-reasons-why-you-need-stronger-authentication-now. Accessed 6 July 2016
4. Boodaei M (2010) Real-time phishing takes off. Security intelligence: analysis and insight for information security professionals. https://securityintelligence.com/real-time-phishing-takes-off/#.VdOTBHhh1Bw. Accessed 6 July 2016
5. Schneier B (2016) Credential stealing as an attack vector. Schneier on Security blog. https://www.schneier.com/blog/archives/2016/05/credential_stea.html. Accessed 6 July 2016
6. Vellon M (2010) Authentication in the cloud. Network World. http://www.networkworld.com/article/2194263/tech-primers/authentication-in-the-cloud.html. Accessed 6 July 2016
7. Dinesha HA, Agrawal VK (2012) Multi-level authentication technique for accessing cloud services ICCCA. doi:10.1109/ICCCA.2012.6179130
8. Schneier B (2016) Google moving towards surveillance. Schneier on Security blog. https://www.schneier.com/blog/archives/2016/05/google_moving_f.html. Accessed 6 July 2016
9. Schneier B (1996) Applied cryptography: protocols, algorithms and source code in C. Wiley, New York
10. OpenID Authentication 2.0 (2007) OpenID Foundation Website. http://openid.net/specs/openid-authentication-2_0.html. Accessed 6 July 2016
11. OAuth 2.0. authorization framework (2012) Internet engineering task force tools http://tools.ietf.org/html/rfc6749. Accessed 6 July 2016
12. Richer J. User authentication with OAuth 2.0. OAuth community website. http://oauth.net/articles/authentication/. Accessed 6 July 2016
13. Kerberos: the network authentication protocol (2016) MIT Website. http://web.mit.edu/kerberos/. Accessed 6 July 2016
14. Harrison R (2006) Lightweight Directory Access Protocol (LDAP): authentication methods and security mechanisms. Internet Engineering Task Force Tools. https://tools.ietf.org/html/rfc4513. Accessed 6 July 2016
15. Biometrics standard ISO19092:2008 security framework (2013) International Organization for Standardization. http://www.iso.org/iso/catalogue_detail?csnumber=50145. Accessed 6 July 2016
16. Grotner P, Salamon W, Chandramouli R (2013) NIST special publication 800-76-2. Biometric specifications for personal identity verification. National Institute Standards and Technology Computer Security Division. http://nvlpubs.nist.gov/nistpubs/SpecialPublications/NIST.SP.800-76-2.pdf. Accessed 6 July 2016
17. Bhargava L, VenkataKiran K (2014) Two end point verification of secure data storage over cloud. IJETT 17(9):450–453
18. Spies T, Schmalz S (2013) Tokenization standard ANSI X9.119 Part 2. Using tokenization methods. Accredited Standards Committee X9 Inc. http://x9.org/wp-content/uploads/2014/01/X9-Tokenization-Webinar-January-2014.pptx. Accessed 6 July 2016

19. Scoping SIG, Tokenization Taskforce, PCI SSC (2011) Information supplement: PCI DSS tokenization guidelines. PCI Security Standards Council. https://www.pcisecuritystandards. org/documents/Tokenization_Guidelines_Info_Supplement.pdf. Accessed 6 July 2016

20. 3DSI staff (2013) Credit card tokenization 101. 3Delta Systems Blog. http://www.3dsi.com/ blog/credit-card-tokenization-101. Accessed 6 July 2016

21. IMPERVA (2015) Man in the Cloud (MITC) attacks. Hacker Intelligence Initiative. https:// www.imperva.com/docs/HII_Man_In_The_Cloud_Attacks.pdf. Accessed 6 July 2016

22. Li-Hsiang Kuo Cracking Credit Card Number Tokenization. http://pages.cs.wisc.edu/~lorderic/ webpage/tokenization-crack.pdf. Accessed 6 July 2016

23. Menezes AJ, van Oorschot PC, Vanstone SA (2001) Handbook of applied cryptography. CRC Press, Boca Raton

24. Schneier B, Ferguson N (2003) Practical cryptography. Wiley, New York

25. ISO/IEC 18033-3: Information technology – Security techniques — Encryption algorithms – Part 3: Block ciphers (2016) International Organization for Standardization. http://www.iso. org/iso/catalogue_detail.htm?csnumber=54531. Accessed 6 July 2016

26. McWilliams G (2011).Hardware AES showdown. Grant McWilliams Blog. http://grantmcwil-liams.com/tech/technology/387-hardware-aes-showdown-via-padlock-vs-intel-aes-ni-vs--amd-hexacore. Accessed 6 July 2016

27. Lucian C (2014) Microsoft continues RC4 encryption phase-out plan with. NET security updates. Computerworld Digital Magazine. http://www.computerworld.com/article/2489395/ encryption/microsoft-continues-rc4-encryption-phase-out-plan-with--net-security-updates. html. Accessed 6 July 2016

28. Bangerter E, Gullasch D, Krenn S (2010) Cache games – bringing access-based cache attacks on AES to practice. Cryptology ePrint Archive. http://eprint.iacr.org/2010/594.pdf. Accessed 6 July 2016

29. Breaking AES-128 in real time, no ciphertext required. Hacker News. https://news.ycombina-tor.com/item?id=1937902. Accessed 6 July 2016

30. Jonsson J, Kaliski B (2003) PKCS standards: RSA cryptography specifications: version 2.1. Engineering Task Force Tools. https://tools.ietf.org/html/rfc3447. Accessed 6 July 2016

31. Brown RL (2009) SEC 1: elliptic curve cryptography. Standards for Efficient Cryptography Group (SECG). http://www.secg.org/sec1-v2.pdf. Accessed 6 July 2016

32. NIST Special publication 800-57 Recommendation for Key Management – Part 1: general (2005) National Institute Standards and Technology Computer Security Division. http://csrc. nist.gov/publications/nistpubs/800-57/sp800-57_part1_rev3_general.pdf. Accessed 6 July 2016

33. Goyal V, Pandey O, Sahai A, Waters B (2006) Attribute-based encryption for fine-grained access control of encrypted data. ACM CCS 06:89–98. doi:10.1145/1180405.1180418

34. Bellovin SM, Merritt M (1993) Augmented encrypted key exchange: a password-based proto-col secure against dictionary attacks and password file compromise. ACM CCS 93:244–250. doi:10.1145/168588.168618

35. Kocher P, Jaffe J, Jun B (1999) Differential power analysis. LNCS 1666:388–397

36. Kocher P, Jaffe J, Jun B, Rohatgi P (2011) Introduction to differential power analysis. J Cryptogr Eng 1:5. doi:10.1007/s13389-011-0006-y

37. Boutin C (2015) NIST releases SHA-3 cryptographic hash standard. NIST Information Technology Laboratory. http://www.nist.gov/itl/csd/201508_sha3.cfm

38. Shamir A (1979) How to share a secret. Commun ACM 22(11):612–613

39. Galibus T, Matveev G, Shenets N (2009) Some structural and security properties of the modu-lar secret sharing. SYNASC 2008:197–200. doi:10.1109/SYNASC.2008.14

40. ANSI ASC X9.95 Standard for Trusted Time Stamps (2012) Accredited Standards Committee X9 Inc. https://x9.org/standards/. Accessed 6 July 2016

41. ISO/IEC 18014 Information technology — Security techniques — Time-stamping services (2014) International Organization for Standardization. http://www.iso.org/iso/home/store/cat-alogue_tc/catalogue_detail.htm?csnumber=50678. Accessed 6 July 2016

42. Yu S, Wang C, Ren K, Lou W (2010) Achieving secure, scalable, and fine-grained data access control in cloud computing. IEEE INFOCOM 2010:534–542

43. Parakh A, Kak S (2009) Online data storage using implicit security. Inform Sci 179:3323–3331

44. Initiative for Open Authentication (2007) OATH reference architecture version 2.0. OATH Initiative Website. https://openauthentication.org/wp-content/uploads/2015/09/Reference ArchitectureVersion2.pdf. Accessed 6 July 2016

45. Hu CV et al (2014) NIST special publication 800-162. Guide to Attribute Based Access Control (ABAC) definition and considerations. National Institute Standards and Technology. http://nvlpubs.nist.gov/nistpubs/SpecialPublications/NIST.SP.800-162.pdf. Accessed 6 July 2016

46. Musa S (2014) Cybersecurity: access control. Evolllution Online Newspaper. http://www. evolllution.com/media_resources/cybersecurity-access-control/. Accessed 6 July 2016

47. Shamir A (1984) Identity-based cryptosystems and signature schemes. LNCS 7:47–53

48. Boneh D, Franklin KM (2001) Identity-based encryption from the weil pairing. LNCS 2139:213–229

49. Storgrid secure enterprise share and sync solution. http://www.storgrid.com/. Accessed 6 July 2016

50. Galibus T, Vissia H (2015) Cloud storage security. Proc NSCE 2014:123–127

51. Alotaibi S, Furnell S, Clarke, N (2015) Transparent authentication systems for mobile device security: a review. 2015 10th international conference for Internet Technology and Secured Transactions (ICITST), London, pp 406–413

52. "TCG Mobile Reference Architecture Specification Version 1.0, Revision 1," June 2008. Available at: http://www.trustedcomputinggroup.org/tcg-mobile-reference-architecture-specification-v1-r5-26-june-2008/

Chapter 4
Cloud Storage Security Architecture

This chapter presents a model and step-by-step systematic construction of the cloud storage protection system. The formal model allows to make the whole process of deploying the security system transparent and easily verifiable. The systematic construction methodology aims to optimize the mechanism selection and control the security at all levels. The mechanisms conform to the attacks and vulnerabilities at each step so that the protection of the whole architecture is provided continuously.

4.1 General Model of the Security System

The security system for cloud storage from the point of deployment and implementation is a set of software components and corresponding databases. The component framework allows to modify or upgrade the corresponding security modules easily. The following model of security component framework begins with the general components and proceeds to specific ones. The developers and system analysts can follow the two-level approach to modeling the security system framework as follows.

Level 1: The General Security Mechanisms
This level includes the mechanisms that are applicable for the whole cloud storage infrastructure. They are:

- *Managing identities*: Identity management (IM) is a set of mechanisms related to the way a user is identified in the system and the way his identity is verified. The processes that are specified in this subsystem are identification and authentication.
- *Access control*: Access control (AC) includes the phase of setting up the security policies and distributing the keys and the process of authorizing the users according to their access rights. Therefore, it includes the concept of access policies

© The Author(s) 2016   69
T. Galibus et al., *Elements of Cloud Storage Security*, SpringerBriefs in
Computer Science, DOI 10.1007/978-3-319-44962-3_4

(see previous chapter), authorization method, and AC mechanism for granting the access.

- *Security policies specification*: This is a specification of user access levels. Each of access levels specified in the system gives rights to specific actions. The security policies (SP) need to conform not only along with the system requirements but also with the current security standards in the country [1, 2]. The security policies should specify how the data is accessed and how far it can be saved in accordance with the security perimeter.

Level 2: The Component-Specific Mechanisms
These are the mechanisms that are supposed to function differently for different components of the cloud storage. In other words, there are different implementations of the same modules for each cloud component.

- *Key distributing and storing*: The key management subsystem (KM) is the most important cryptographic module from the point of security [3]. It includes the procedures of key generation, key exchange, key distribution, key storing, key renovation, revocation, etc.
- *Data encryption method*: The data encryption (DE) mechanism supports the data confidentiality and accessibility. It should be implemented separately for different storage components.
- *Threat intelligence and audit*: TI subsystem includes the methods of collecting the user-specific data, reporting, and analyzing the user activities.
- *Usage of tokens*: The token management (TM) module defines the token generation and management procedures. This is a separate set of procedures related to security due to the growth of attacks on this function (see previous chapter).

This model is summarized in Fig. 4.1.

In other words, the construction of a security system includes specification of general mechanisms and the specification of component-specific ones. It is obvious that the system construction starts from the general ones. In practice, the methodology of construction does not completely follow the model because some steps in the level 1 require the level 2 elements. The next section outlines the step-by-step construction algorithm.

Fig. 4.1 Cloud storage security model

4.2 Step-by-Step Security System Construction

The methodology of SS construction follows the proposed SS model. It starts from the IM subsystem, which might require specification of additional token management (TM), data encryption (DE), and key management (KM) services.

- *Step 1. Construction of identity management infrastructure*

The IMI is introduced as a core of the security framework. It includes the IM module or a method of identifying and authenticating the users. Also, it includes the TM module in order to provide the support to authentication when the user is logged into the system. In other words, it provides a base of managing the user identity. The interconnected mechanisms on levels 1 and 2 are constructed simultaneously.

The construction of security infrastructure includes the following procedures:

- Specifying user identities
- Setting up the authentication method
- Setting up the token management (TM) module

Note that this stage does not require any cryptography. It serves for detecting and verifying the user. The tokens have to be specified in order to support the user identity on later stages and to improve the usability of the system.

- *Step 2. Construction of access control framework*

This is an essential step for a corporate cloud storage. In a protected cloud with a centralized authority, granting access to the data deployment of the AC subsystem is the most important and complex procedure. Before setting up the authorization service, one is supposed to set up the appropriate KM and DE modules. The construction of ACF includes:

- Setting up the authorization policies: data access levels and security levels
- Setting up the KM and DE authorization modules with respect to the access policies
- Specifying the user groups and their respective shares
- Setting up the group user keys for the data access
- Distributing the group user keys
- Granting access and managing the authorization keys
- Managing the key revocation and key renewal procedures

Note that the KM system cannot be specified unless the authorization policies are defined. The authorization policy specifies the way of using the attributes and the respective algorithm of user key generation (see Sect. 3.3). For simple selective policies, the simplified algorithm can be used. KM system should be configured before the authorization setup. The authorization functions are a vital part of the whole lifecycle of a cloud storage and require a special attention.

- *Step 3. Identification of the component security*

This step specifies the configuration of the security mechanisms for each component of the cloud storage.

- Security on a server:

  - Setting up the server storage security:

    1. Configuring the KM and DE modules in accordance with the server requirements
    2. Setting up the protected key storage
    3. Setting up the appropriate re-encryption method

  - Setting up the data transition security:

    1. Configuring the KM and DE modules for the data in transit
    2. Setting up the respective key storage
    3. Setting up key renovation method

- Security on a client:

  - Setting up the client storage security:

    1. Configuring the KM and DE modules in accordance with the client requirements
    2. Setting up the protected key storage

  - Setting up the data transition security:

    1. Configuring the KM and DE modules for the data in transit
    2. Setting up the respective key storage

  - Setting up the data in use security:

    1. Configuring the protected memory usage

- Security on a mobile device:

  - Setting up the mobile storage security:

    1. Configuring the KM and DE modules in accordance with the mobile requirements
    2. Setting up the protected key storage

  - Setting up the data transition security:

    1. Configuring the KM and DE modules for the data in transit
    2. Setting up the respective key storage

  - Setting up the data in use security:

    1. Configuring the protected memory usage

  - Setting up the protection in the offline mode

- *Step 4. Construction of threat intelligence unit*

The threat intelligence module includes the monitoring, reporting, and analysis of user activities. It includes all audit and logging operations in the system. It is recommended to configure the basic TI for the portable devices and clients in the cloud storage. TI obviously cannot function without the security infrastructure setup as the user identity should be known and the authorization as the access rights should be defined. It includes:

- Monitoring basic activities on a mobile
- Monitoring basic activities on client computer
- Reporting and analysis of basic activities
- Monitoring and analysis of specific activities

First of all, TI unit should support the monitoring of the most important activities such as user login and counting of failed tries, data request and upload frequency, and location change. These basic operations help to prevent many threats such as ransomware or DDoS attacks (see Chap. 2).

- *Step 5. Verification and optimization*

After the construction phase, the security framework is supposed to be verified, tested, and reconfigured if necessary. The optimization is a continuous process providing a more efficient usage of the organization resources, improved security, and efficiency of the system operation. The methods used for optimization are:

- Detection of the neutralized attacks
- Adding the required mechanisms
- Reducing the excessive mechanisms
- Analysis of the most time-consuming operations and their reduction

The proposed methodology approaches the security system construction as a sequence of the logically interconnected steps. The order of the construction steps of this section can be summarized in Fig. 4.2.

Fig. 4.2   The construction of security framework

4.3 Identification of the Identity Management Infrastructure

4.3.1 Formal Model of Identity Management Infrastructure

Managing user identities is mandatory for any secured information system [4]. In the cloud-based environment, such as protected storage, setting up the identities is a key step of the security management.

The complete control of the confidential data can never be guaranteed in the cloud as the cloud is never completely centralized and due to virtualization and transparency does not have a stable security perimeter. The establishment of secure communication and data exchange requires the extensive use of cryptographic methods.

Note: *Authentication, i.e., specifying and verifying who the user is, requires setting up the tokenization mechanism because the tokens serve to authenticate the user in later communication stages. Authentication does not require cryptographic methods once cryptography cannot guarantee the user identity; it verifies the validity of the key or the use possession of the key.*

The complete process of setting up the authentication and tokenization is introduced as the identity management infrastructure (IMI) in order to highlight the initial stage of the security configuration and to produce a coherent model of the interconnected security mechanisms: authentication, identification, and token management (Fig. 4.3).

The user operations that are specified on this stage are:

1. *User registration* includes identification and authentication setup.
2. *User login* includes authentication and token generation.
3. *User operation while logged in* includes token usage.

The first procedure is run only once for each user in the system. The second procedure always precedes the third one. The third one is run multiple times, i.e., every time a user session is established via a second procedure (Fig. 4.4).

Fig. 4.3 Identity management infrastructure

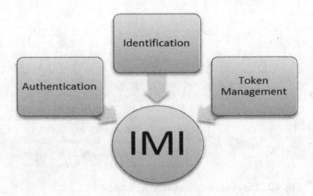

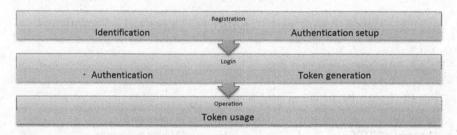

Fig. 4.4 Identity management workflow

4.3.2   Types of IMI in Relation to Cloud Storages

The following types of authentication can be applied to the cloud storages (see Sect. 3.1):

- *LA+Auth1*: local one-factor authentication
- *LA+AuthM*: local multifactor authentication
- *RA+Auth1*: remote one-factor authentication
- *RA+AuthM*: remote multifactor authentication

The security of the authentication method increases from *LA+Auth1* to *RA+AuthM*. The multifactor authentication can be performed by means of SMS, biometric information API, etc. The constant PIN added to the user password does not provide the second authentication factor. The second factor that can be verified is the user ownership of the mobile device, location, possession of a smart card, fingerprints, etc. For the security purposes, it is not recommended to use LA for the corporate storages due to high risk of leakage so this option is omitted in the proposed solutions.

The tokens to be used to secure the communication with the server are generated from user password and device ID in order to verify the possession of a device:

1. User password-based token (UT)
2. Pass+device-based token (UDT)
3. No token (NoT)

Additionally, a PIN code can be set up in order to enhance the token usage security and protect from MiTM/MiTC attacks (see Chap. 2):

1. One-time PIN (OTP)
2. No PIN (NoP)
3. Constant PIN (CP)

The security of the token generation can be illustrated by the following chart where the less secure solutions precede the more secure ones (Fig. 4.5).

The presence of an additional PIN is more important for the security than the token usage, because it is a second source of user identification data that is constantly verified. Tokens are compromised by means of many common cloud storage attacks

Fig. 4.5 Token generation security chart

Table 4.1 Types of IMI for various cloud storages

Type of IMI	Cost	Time	Security	Type of cloud
RA+Auth1 + UDT/CP	1	1	1	Minimized security
				Smaller company
				Fast deployment
RA+AuthM+NoP	2	2	2	Acceptable security
				Middle-size company
				Average deployment
RA+AuthM+UDT/CP	2	2	3	Acceptable security
				Middle-size company
				Average deployment
RA+AuthM+UDT/OTP	3	2	4	Middle/big company
				Extremely protected storage
				Unlimited deployment resources

such as MiTM and MiTC (see Chap. 2). One-time PIN is a particular type of token that can increase security if:

1. It is generated on a server and sent over to user for the period of session via SMS, i.e., establishing a two-factor authentication.
2. It is generated independently on a client and server as series of sequential hashes, i.e., hash chains or Merkle trees similar to trusted timestamping [5].

To conclude the subsection, the following IMI types can be considered in practice:

1. RA+Auth1+UDT/CP
2. RA+AuthM+NoP
3. RA+AuthM+UDT/CP
4. RA+AuthM+UDT/OTP

Each type of IMI has its advantages and disadvantages and is more suitable for particular types of systems. In practice, the token generation based on both user and device ID is more secure but is not difficult to implement; in all cases, it is a preferable tokenization type. One-time PIN system is more costly to deploy and requires a special API. The connection of the type of IMI and the type of cloud storage can be illustrated by Table 4.1.

4.3.3   Proposed Authentication Solutions

The above analysis shows that a corporate cloud for most companies with confidential data to be protected requires the following key features in the authentication process:

1. The usage of a strong password
2. Third-party authentication
3. Two-factor/strong authentication
4. Additional endpoint authentication to verify the device in the BYOD environment (token)
5. Continuous user credentials verification (token and PIN)

Based on the analysis, several basic strategies are proposed for the deployment and implementation of the authentication protocol. The proposed solutions are optimized for the corporate clouds.

The following solution is implemented in the protected cloud storage [6]. Unlike Google or Dropbox, it uses the additional PIN verification in order to enhance the usage of tokens. PIN is a fast and easily deployed solution to support the device security in the BYOD environment.

Solution 4.1: The Cloud Solution for Authentication – Protocol STR

1. User enters his credentials. Strong password is used.
2. The token is generated for the user session with the help of device ID and user credentials.
3. This token is sent to server via secured protocol.
4. The server verifies the token and asks user PIN (that was generated before and sent to user via email).
5. User is requested to enter a PIN additionally every 5 min the device is not used.

Usage of one-time PIN sent by SMS makes the system infeasible. The renewal of PIN in every session corresponds to the well-known standard of smart card protection (PCI-DSS) [7].

Solution 4.2: The Cloud Solution for Authentication – Protocol STR-SMSPIN

1. User enters his credentials. Strong password is used.
2. The token is generated for the user session with the help of device ID and user credentials.
3. This token is sent to server via secured protocol.
4. The server verifies the token and generates a one-time PIN (optionally).
5. The PIN is sent via SMS.
6. User enters PIN and continues the session.
7. Every 5 min device is not used, the resending of one-time PIN is required.

The above are based on the following software components:

- Token generation – on a device and server
- Token verification – server
- PIN generation – server
- PIN sending via SMS – server
- Timer counter to enter PIN – device

From the complexity point of view, all operations to be implemented are not time-consuming. The most time-consuming operation in the whole infrastructure is hashing and it requires just a minimum load on the system (see Sect. 3.2).

4.4 Identification of Access Control Framework

Access control framework (ACF) is a crucial security component for a corporate storage [8]. ACF includes the configuration of security policies and specific access rules. The key revocation and renewal are the most vulnerable procedures being the source of confidential data leakage in the big companies. Organization of the ACF requires the following steps.

4.4.1 Setting Up Security Policies

The specification of ACF begins with the access and security policies setup. The security policies are divided into three groups:

- Data confidentiality levels
- Attribute or group authorization policies
- Security perimeter encryption policies

1. *Data confidentiality levels*

The data confidentiality levels define the correspondence of access rights and data availability. They are specified according to the level of information security supported by a company and the national security standard [1]. For the usability purposes, the confidentiality levels in the cloud storage should not exceed four. In practice, the following recommendations can be accepted:

1. For small companies: open/restricted (two levels)
2. For medium companies: open/restricted/confidential (three levels)
3. For big companies or for companies with highly sensitive data: open/restricted/confidential/highly secured (four levels)

2. *User access policies*

The access policies for the users specify the way the attributes and user groups are organized in a company. The groups can be set up hierarchically or can be specified directly or use specific attribute subsets. The particular type of access policy depends on the organization type.

1. *Group policy*

This is the simplest and most convenient way to organize the access policy in any organization. The groups are specified as subsets of users directly. The access rights to specific file shares are specified as a set of related groups.

Example Let Group1 = {User1, User2, User3}, Group2 = {User2, User3, User4}, Group3 = {User4}. Then the access to the shares is specified by the relation: Share1 = {Group1, Group4}, Share2 = {Group1, Group2}. These relations specify that all users User1, User2, User3, User4 have access to both shares.

2. *Hierarchy policy*

If a particular organization has more than three levels of hierarchy, it might be efficient to set up a hierarchy policy. It is almost similar to the group policy with a deeper structure of subgroups.

Example Let Group1 = {User1, User2, User3, User4}, Group2 = {User2, User3, User4}, Group3 = {User3, User4}. Let the hierarchy levels be 1, 2, 3. Let Group1Level = 1, Group2Level = 2, Group3Level = 3. Then the shares Share1 = {1} and Share2 = {3} specify that all users in Group1 have access to Share1 and only the users in Group3 have access Share2.

3. *General attribute policy*

If there are many complex intersections in an organization, i.e., a user should belong to several groups in order to be eligible to access the share a general attribute policy should be used. In this case, some share is accessible for the members of two or more groups.

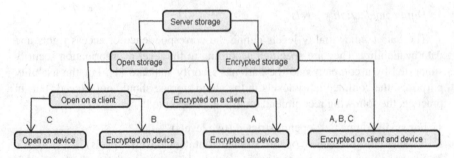

Fig. 4.6 Security perimeter policies

Example Let Group1 = {User1, User2, User3}, Group2 = {User2, User3, User4}, Group3 = {User4}. Then the access to the share specified by Share1 = {{Group1 AND Group2}, Group3}, authorizes User2, User3, User4 to have access to share.

3. *Security perimeter policy*

The security perimeter policy specifies whether the data should be encrypted when it is transferred to a less protected storage component, i.e., client computer or portable device. The security perimeter policy depends on the amount of confidential data transferred and the level of data confidentiality in a company. The data stored on a server is divided into open and encrypted storage. When a particular share is transferred to a client or a portable device, it can be encrypted for protection or kept in clear (Fig. 4.6).

The diagram shows the possible levels of security perimeter policies that can be set up for different organizations:

- *Type A*: highly confidential documents
- *Type B*: restricted documents that are accessible only on a server
- *Type C*: important company documents that require authorization to be accessed and therefore should be encrypted on a device
- *Type D*: documents without access limitations

In most scenarios, the security perimeter levels correspond to the levels of confidentiality.

The proposed recommendation is:

1. Company with two confidentiality levels: C, D or B, C
2. Company with three confidentiality levels: A, B, C or B, C, D
3. Company with four confidentiality levels: A, B, C, D or A, B, C

The chart summarizes the results of this section (Fig. 4.7).

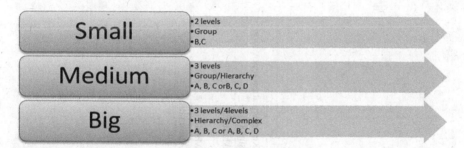

Fig. 4.7 Cloud storage scenarios and security policies

4.4.2   Configuring the Data Encryption

In order to set up the authorization in the cloud storage, one has to configure the respective data encryption (DE) and key management (KM) modules. As it is mentioned in Sect. 3.3, the DE methods that are used in the procedure of authorization are PKE with manual attribute setting, IBE and ABE. The comparative security of all these methods is based on one of the selected PKE security (see Sect. 3.2). The complexity of implementation differs.

For small companies with less complex structure, manual configuration is easier to organize and control. For a medium/big company with more prominent dynamics in user attributes and access rights or with a larger number of users to maintain, it is preferable to implement an ABE/IBE in order to reduce the attribute matching procedures. To conclude, PKE with manual attribute matching is easier to implement, but ABE/IBE is easier to use because the attributes are generated automatically to match the user access rights and policies. Table 4.2 presents the analysis of different authorization methods.

Setting up attribute-based encryption is a recommended strategy for most medium/big companies. The advantages of such solution are mentioned in the table though the implementation might be time-consuming (see Sect. 3.3). Once the data encryption method is selected, the appropriate procedures are to be implemented:

- Initialization of attributes
- Key generation procedure
- Encryption procedure
- Decryption procedure

The *initialization of attributes* can be implemented in two ways:

1. Generate all necessary attributes for the existing user groups and shares and add the new attributes once the new groups are added to the organization.
2. The excessive number of attributes can be generated in the initial phase. The attributes are used once the new groups are added.

The correspondence of groups and group attributes is then stored in the database on a server.

Table 4.2 Analysis of authorization methods

Authorization method	Company size	Difficulty of implementation	Difficulty of usage	Group complexity and hierarchy	Dynamics of users and attributes	Key revocation/renovation support
PKE with manual attributes	Small/medium	Low	High	Low	Low	Manual
IBE	Big/medium	Middle	Middle	Middle	Middle	Manual
ABE	Big/medium	High	Low	High	High	Automatic

The key generation procedure requires the setup for shares and groups. After that, the encryption and decryption procedures can be implemented (the algorithm is outlined in Sect. 3.3).

4.4.3   Configuring Key Management

The corporate cloud storage authorization procedure requires a centralized authority to set up the attributes and generate the keys. It is important to implement a set of complementary key management methods in order to provide a sufficient support of authorization security:

- Key distribution
- Key revocation
- Key renovation
- Key storing

The *key renovation and revocation* methods are discussed in Sect. 3.3 and are specified within the authorization implementation. As it is mentioned in Table 4.2, ABE is more suitable method for providing the adequate support for these procedures.

The *key distribution* methods are based on AES encryption with the temporary key or public-key encryption with a constant private key. The temporary or constant key can be complemented with user login and PIN. Additionally, secret sharing scheme can be used to enhance the security of key transportation. If there are sufficient resources, encrypted key exchange can be implemented (see Sect. 3.2). Figure 4.8 illustrates the security of the proposed methods.

As one can see from the diagram, the security of distribution of the authorization key is defined by the generation of temporary or constant key used for the distribu-

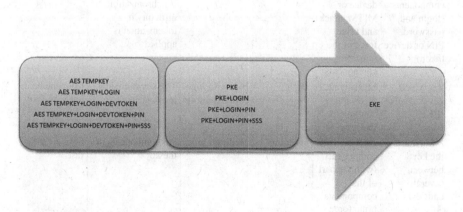

Fig. 4.8 Security of the key distribution

tion. The encryption method is symmetric or asymmetric. The security increases with the number of components used to compose the distribution key. The secret sharing allows to provide the sufficient security even if some the components are revealed to the adversary. The most secure method of key distribution is encrypted key exchange [9]. It requires more time and resources for the implementation.

The strategy for selection of a specific key distribution method depends on several factors:

- Complexity of implementation
- Efficiency of usage
- Attacks and vulnerabilities

Table 4.3 The characteristics of key distribution

Type of KD scheme	Attacks	Complexity of realization	Types of clouds	Vulnerabilities	Efficiency of usage
AES with temporary key generated on server	Man in the middle attack, masquerade	Low	Small, with minimum protection level	The seed of key generating function is sent over unprotected network, synchronization difficulty if tokenization is applied	Fast and convenient
PKE with constant key stored on a device	Attack on a device, masquerade	Low	Small, with limited amount of portable devices	The memory on a device or the portable device	Convenient, not very fast
AES generated with the use of additional components (login and password, PIN or device token)	Attack on part of the components (user data, device or MITM attack) and brute force of the remaining components	Medium	Medium, big	The network or device or user data (login and password and PIN), synchronization difficulty if tokenization is applied	Fast and convenient
Encrypted key exchange (EKE)	Masquerade of several continuous messages	High	Big, with high confidentiality level	The key exchange messages	Convenient, not very fast
SSS (sharing the key between several entities)	Attack on all components (with the part of the components brute force attack is not effective)	Medium	Medium, big	All components of the key	Convenient, fast

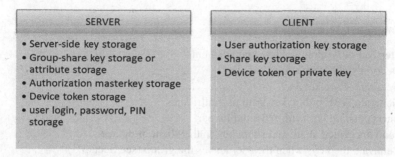

Fig. 4.9 Key storage structure

Table 4.3 illustrates the characteristics of the basic key distribution methods.

The key storage should be organized in a protected memory of the device and the keys are to be removed from the RAM after usage. In order to enhance the key revocation, the authorization keys on a server are to be stored in a separate storage. The recommended key storage structure is as follows (Fig. 4.9).

The storages are to be stored in a protected memory and protected:

- *Server-side key storage* is protected by the administrator master key (see Sect. 3.2).
- *Group-share key storage* is public.
- *Authorization master key and the storage of user logins, passwords, and PINs* are protected by administrator master key.
- *User authorization key storage* is protected by the user password, PIN, and device token.
- *Share key storage* is protected by user authorization keys.
- *Device token or private key* is protected by the user password and PIN.

The recommendations and strategies of this section can be summarized in the following authorization protocol.

Solution 4.3: Authorization Protocol ABE-STR

Step 1: Configuration of security policies
Set up security policy: group access policy, three levels of confidentiality, security perimeter policy type A
Step 2: Initialization (see Sect. 3.3)
Generate attributes
Set up group-share attributes
Set up master key
Save master key in a protected storage
Generate attribute-based keys
Distribute authorization keys using the AES key generated from the temporary or constant user token and/or secret sharing scheme (see Sect. 3.3).

(continued)

Solution 4.3 (continued)

Step 3: Encryption and key management
Decrypt share with server-side key.
Generate share key.
Generate ABE public key with user attributes.
Encrypt share key with ABE public part.
Send encrypted share and share key to the client or device.
Renovate the keys when the user leaves the group (see Sect. 3.3).
Renovate keys when they expire (see Sect. 3.3).
Generate new keys when group is added.

4.5   Identification of Threat Intelligence Unit

The threat intelligence unit defines the reporting and analysis procedures of user activities in the cloud storage. The CASB system can be installed in the system in order to organize the reporting of the activities [10, 11]. Most CASB are unfortunately based on the minimum analysis of the activities but collect the excessive data of user activities, which is often difficult to analyze. The correlation and regression methods based on the advanced mathematical models such as MOS [12] can provide a better security in the case of DDoS and ransomware attacks and automate the maintenance of a cloud storage without putting excessive load on the network. Such custom designed and implemented methods and algorithms of data analysis prove to be more effective but require more time for implementation and deployment.

It is recommended to arrange the minimal reporting unit even for the small companies because this allows to easily prevent the common attacks and threats such as ransomware and MITC (see Chap. 2 for detailed attack description). Table 4.4 illustrates the strategy of organizing the TIU.

The details of the TIU organization are outlined in Sect. 3.4.

4.6   Identification of the Component Security Framework

The components of a cloud storage are server, client, and mobile device data storages apart from the data transfer channels and storage-related processes. Each of the components requires a specific strategy in order to organize the optimized protection system configured according to the component role and function. As the general security mechanisms are set up, it is possible to organize the data protection for every cloud component separately.

Table 4.4   Analysis of TIU implementation

Type of TIU	Type of cloud storage	Activities to be reported	Special features
Basic reporting	Small with basic security	User uploading, downloading modifying shares	If the time between the uploads/downloads is too small, it can be a ransomware attack
Basic reporting and restricted analysis	Small or medium with acceptable security level	User uploading, downloading modifying shares, user incorrect login or PIN, user changing access right	The failed tries should be counted
			The revocation should be reported
CASB-based advanced reporting	Big with sufficient resources	All user and server activities are reported and visualized	The suspicious activities apart from above include the change of location or any activity that is beyond normal
Using advanced mathematical models and decision-making methods	Medium to big with a high security level	All user and server activities are used for the data analysis and decision making	The frequency of activities can be analyzed, the contents of file contents, the suspicious activities can be used for the further analysis

4.6.1   The Basic Strategies to Organize the Server Protected Storage

As it is mentioned in the previous chapter, the server-side protection should provide the security for the following processes:

1. Security at rest: encryption, key management, and reporting
2. Security in transit: encryption, key management, and reporting

It is recommended to consider the following basic protocol for server-side data at rest security.

Solution 4.4: Server Side at Rest Data Protection
Select the files to be stored in the protected storage/open storage. The selection is based on the confidentiality policy, confidentiality labels, and the setup of server-side data protection threshold.
Use an efficient symmetric encryption method (AES256, Blowfish, Serpent, IDEA) to encrypt the protected storage.
Renew the symmetric keys periodically and re-encrypt the data storage.
Organize a protected key storage

(continued)

Solution 4.4 (continued)

Store the data key in a separate protected storage. Administrator owns a key
    storage master key.
Use secret sharing to protect the key storage key. Part of the key is protected
    by administrator password and another part is owned by administrator.
Store the master key on a flash drive.
Organize a protected key storage re-encryption process.
Use a newly generated session key for each user while sending a file to a user.
Report and analyze all the operations in protected storage:

  Decryption.
  Encryption and saving.
  Storage re-encryption.
  Key generation or sharing.

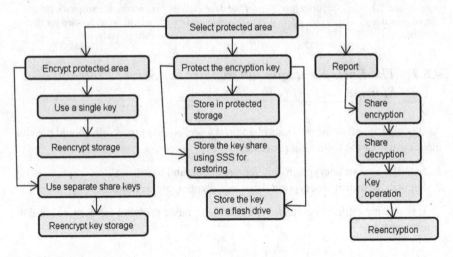

Fig. 4.10 Server-side data at rest security

The solution is illustrated in Fig. 4.10.
The security of data in transit at server side requires a special attention because
operation often becomes a source of vulnerabilities and attacks.

- According to Sect. 3.3, the attribute-based encryption or some other access control method should be configured on a server in order to authorize users. The
  access control keys can be either constant or expiring.
- The expiry period can be regular or related to the key revocation operation, i.e.,
  a user leaving the organization. In practice, the regular expiry period is easier to
  maintain.

- The authorization key transport should be protected on the server and client side. Server ensures that the user is correctly authenticated.
- It is preferable that the share is encrypted with a symmetric encryption and ABE is used to protect a share key.

The most demanding security configuration scenario involves four processes. The recommended solution includes all these steps. Some of them can be omitted in practice.

Solution 4.5: Server-Side Data in Transit Security

Receive user credentials (password and login).
Check user credentials.
If credentials are okay.
Generate device token if necessary for the further communication.
Send the share list and device token to user.
Check hashed timestamp if the authorization keys have expiry period.
If there is no need to renovate the authorization keys.
Receive the user request.
Check the device token received along with the request.
Generate AES share key.
Decrypt file from the storage.
Encrypt the AES key with authorization key.
Encrypt the share with AES key.
Delete AES key.
Send share and key to user.
If it is necessary to renovate the key.
Generate the user authorization keys on server.
Use the key transport method to encrypt the keys.
Send the keys to user.
Receive share modifications from user.
If the frequency is okay.
Check the device token.
Perform virus check.
Encrypt the modified share.
Save it in the protected storage instead of the same share.
Produce reports on the share synchronization and share list sending.
Block the device after three incorrect tries of entering user credentials.

Figure 4.11 illustrates the above data in transit protection protocol.

Some of these steps can be omitted. But for any cloud storage, it is necessary to provide a secured key distribution mechanism and hybrid encryption to encrypt the share and support attribute-based authorization.

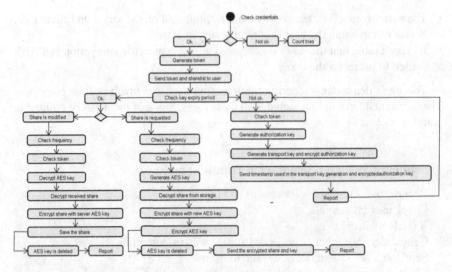

Fig. 4.11 Server-side data in transit protection

4.6.2 The Basic Strategies to Secure the Client Application

The data on a client should be protected in use, in transit, at rest, and when it leaves the premises of organization.

Data in transit: The guidelines for organizing the data in transit protection on a client are contained in Fig. 4.11 for the server-side data in transit protection.

Data leaving the premises: This should not be permitted in the case of highly sensitive data. The modification should be reported, and the synchronized modified file should be kept in clear or in quarantine.

Data in use is protected via the client application user interface and obfuscation procedures:

- The decrypted file is stored in the protected memory.
- Application provides the limited editing capabilities.
- The file storage is separated from the keys.
- Keys are stored in protected memory.
- Reporting is organized.
- Keys are erased after usage.

Data at rest is protected with the AES encryption. AES key is stored in a protected memory and encrypted with ABE.

The mobile device protection recommendations are similar to the general client protection strategy. The important additions are:

- Enhanced protection at minimal resource cost.
- The implementation of PIN verification when the device is in idle or after every share request.

- As the portable device can leave the organization premises, there should be an additional strategy of offline mode protection (see Sect. 3.5).
- The reporting and analysis should be reduced due to the resource limitations.

4.7 Security Optimization and Verification

It is important to provide the transparent verification procedure for the selected security architecture. The checklist of the expected attacks should be verified against the list of attacks neutralized by the specific mechanisms and groups of security components (see Chaps. 2 and 3). Additional verification can be performed for the list of protected channels and processes in the cloud storage.

4.7.1 Attack Prevention Verification

The attacks are classified according to the cloud component and the company size, presented in Table 4.5.

The set of selected security mechanisms and the neutralized attacks is to be verified against the above table. After that the mechanisms can be implemented in order to neutralize the most important attacks out of those that are left unattended. The importance of attacks is based on the evaluation performed by the security experts. The attacks in the table above are listed in the order of importance according to the recommendations and experience of the authors.

4.7.2 Component Security Testing

When the security framework is tested, it is impossible to verify the protection level of separate components. Therefore, the checklist for the security testing consists of the system channels and processes. Each channel and process protection procedure is to be tested and approbated (Table 4.6).

4.7.3 Security Optimization

The security mechanisms often are time-consuming to implement or require extensive enterprise resources. The constructed model should be optimized in the process of implementation and testing. The common optimization points are:

Table 4.5 The list of attacks classified according to cloud components and types

Cloud storage type	Server attacks	Client attacks/mobile attacks
Small	Submitting a corrupted share file	Submitting a corrupted share
	Submitting a virus	A virus attack
	Attack on administrator master key	Attack on a user password
	~~Attack on a key storage~~	Attack on a user token
	~~Attack on a protected storage~~	~~Attack on user authorization keys~~
	Virus attack via network	Stealing the device
	~~DDoS attack via network~~	~~Attack on a PIN~~
	Ransomware attack	~~Reverse engineering~~
	A corrupted client	Attack on client application
		~~Attack on encrypted share~~
Medium	Submitting a corrupted share file	Submitting a corrupted share
	Submitting a virus	A virus attack
	Attack on administrator master key	Attack on a user password
	Attack on a key storage	Attack on a user token
	Attack on a protected storage	~~Attack on user authorization keys~~
	Virus attack via network	Stealing the device
	~~DDoS attack via network~~	Attack on a PIN
	Ransomware attack	Reverse engineering
	A corrupted client	Attack on client application
		~~Attack on encrypted share~~
Big	Submitting a corrupted share file	Submitting a corrupted share
	Submitting a virus	A virus attack
	Attack on administrator master key	Attack on a user password
	Attack on a key storage	Attack on a user token
	Attack on a protected storage	Attack on user authorization keys
	Virus attack via network	Stealing the device
	DDoS attack via network	Attack on a PIN
	Ransomware attack	Reverse engineering
	A corrupted client	Attack on client application
		Attack on encrypted share

1. Re-encryption process
   The frequent re-encryption procedure can put an additional overhead on the system. In most real-life systems it can be performed once a month. Also, reducing the amount of data being re-encrypted, i.e., re-encrypting the keys instead of the storage, reduces the overload. Re-encryption is not effective against the brute force attack on a stolen data.
2. Reporting procedure
   The excessive reporting is often misleading for the administrator. While the operations should be logged, it is important to analyze only the most vulnerable activities such as the frequency of user operations, access from unusual points, and failed tries.

Table 4.6 Security testing checklist

Channels	Processes
Server2Client	Server
Send user key	Storing the protected data
Send share list	Storing the open data
Send share	Storing the keys
Send share key	Re-encryption
Send token	Storing the master key
Client2Server	Storing the attributes
Send user credentials	Verifying the user data
Send PIN	Generating the authorization keys
Send token	Generating the token
Send encrypted share key	Generating the key for key distribution
Send request for share	Generating the master key
Send modified share	Deleting the expired keys
Send report	Key revocation
	Attribute changing
	Reporting and analysing
	Client
	Generating the key storage key from token
	Restoring the distributed key by means of SS
	Decrypting the share key
	Viewing the permitted share list
	Decrypting the share
	Viewing the share in protected mode
	Modifying the share if permitted
	Denying access if the key is expired
	Deleting the unused info
	Asking for password and PIN
	Counting failed tries
	Report and analysis
	Storing the shares and keys

3. Renovation of the user keys

   The user keys expiry period can be longer if there are too many users and the server and network traffic experiences difficulties due to the overload.

4. Simplification of the solution model

   The proposed mechanism composition for the cloud storage type can be optimized with regard to confidentiality levels, attacks neutralization, and the cost of solution.

4.8   The Practical Implementation

In this section, the three basic security framework implementation scenarios, namely, the security framework for the small, medium, and big company, are proposed. An optimized set of mechanisms and practices is suggested for each scenario.

Scenario 4.1: Small Company
The properties of the solution:

1. Two levels of data confidentiality (open and protected).
2. Number of people is up to 20, one administrator.
3. Information is accessible by two to three groups in company (a simple group hierarchy).

The proposed security mechanisms are:

1. *IMI*: *RA+Auth1 + UDT/CP*: one-factor remote authentication with token generated from user data and device. Additionally a PIN check on a mobile can be performed.
2. ACF:

   - *Policy setup*: Group hierarchy with two levels of confidentiality and files are stored open and encrypted on a server and mobile device and/or a client simultaneously. Manual access control encryption with the correspondence of user attributes and keys stored in the table on a server.
   - *KM and DE setup*: The keys to the user data are to be generated on a client. The private ECDSA keys are protected with AES key generated from the user token. It is requested to renew the password or regenerate the token periodically. The server stores the correspondence of users and groups in a table.
   - *Revocation*: Once a user leaves a group, the table record is deleted.

3. *Reporting*. It is suggested to report the location change, excessive upload or download of the files, and excessive tries to log in.
4. Component security:

   - *Server – Data at rest*: Server is protected by an expiring administrator password. The encrypted storage is protected with AES, and the master key to the key storage is protected with a password. *Data in transit*: Once the data is sent to client or mobile, it is encrypted with AES and AES key is protected with ECDSA public key.
   - *Client – Data at rest*: Protected with the AES, the AES key is protected with the private ECDSA, and the ECDSA key is accessible only with a password. The copy of ECDSA belongs to the device/client computer so the data cannot be accessed from other computer. *Data in use*: In the easiest scenario and the most protected in is not allowed to modify the protected data. The modified data is stored in the open server storage. *Data leaving the premises*: Offline protection is difficult to manage so it should not be allowed.

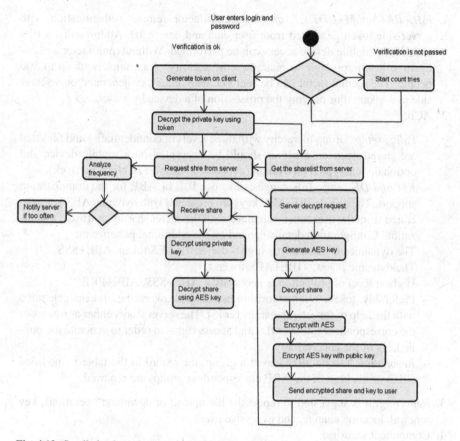

Fig. 4.12 Small cloud storage security architecture

Additionally, it is suggested:

1. Perform re-encryption on a server once a month. Use separate keys for the protected shares on a server and organize a key storage.
2. Encourage users to change password once a month.
3. Use PIN for mobile devices.

The system client workflow can be summarized in Fig. 4.12.

Scenario 4.2: Medium Company
The properties of the solution:

1. Three levels of data confidentiality (open and protected)
2. Number of people is up to 500, several trusted administrators
3. Information is accessible within a simple group hierarchy

The proposed security mechanisms are more specific than those used for a previous scenario:

1. *IMI*: *RA+AuthM+UDT/CP or NoP*: multifactor remote authentication with server-side token generated from user data and device ID. Additionally, a PIN check for a mobile device access can be performed. Without multifactor authentication, it is impossible to guarantee the security of a company of up to 500 people. The second factor can be sent via SMS, email, or generated on a server side as a token, thus proving the possession of a device by a user.

2. ACF:

   - *Policy setup*: Group hierarchy with three levels of confidentiality and files that are stored open on a server should be encrypted on a mobile device and optionally encrypted on a client (depends on the size of client network).
   - *KM and DE setup*: It is suggested to use IBE or ABE for the authorization support. The private IBE/ABE keys are protected with dynamic AES key generated from the user token enhanced with the secret sharing or trusted tokenization. Configuration details depend on the additional parameters:
   - The dynamics in company is high – use ABE+AES/token, ABE+SSS.
   - The dynamic is low – IBE+AES/token.
   - Highest level of protection is necessary – ABE+SSS, ABE+PKE.
   - Preferably, tokenization algorithm uses linked tokens, i.e., tokens generated with the help of timestamp parameter [5]. The server stores either attributes or the correspondence of user IDs and access rights in order to generate the public keys of the encryption.
   - *Revocation*: Once a user leaves a group, the record in the table is modified (IBE) or the keys of the ABE corresponding groups are renewed.

3. *Reporting*. It is suggested to report the file upload or download operations, key renewal, location change, and excessive tries.

4. Component security:

   - *Server – Data at rest*: Server is protected by expiring administrator password. The encrypted storage is protected with separate AES keys for various shares, and the master key to the key storage is protected with a password. If the enhanced security is required, the SSS scheme is used to store the master key. The share of the master key is kept on a flash drive or protected by PIN of administrator's smartphone. *Data in transit*: Once the data is sent to client or mobile, it is encrypted with AES and AES key is protected with ABE/IBE public key.
   - *Client – Data at rest*: Protected with the AES encryption, the key of AES is protected with the private IBE/ABE, and the IBE/ABE key is accessible only via dynamic token (AES key)/SSS share/PKE private key. The share/private key/token belongs to the device/client computer so the data cannot be accessed from other computer and by another user. *Data in use*: It is allowed to modify the data only from the open storage on a client. The protected data modification is restricted. The data cannot be modified or saved outside the client application. *Data leaving the premises*: The data outside the client control zone is considered compromised and cannot be synchronized with the pro-

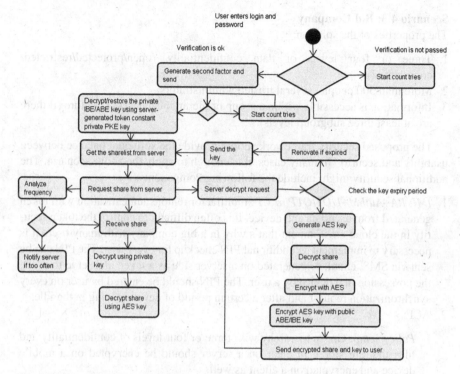

Fig. 4.13 The workflow for a medium size storage client

tected storage on a server. This data either can be synchronized with the open storage or left without possibility to synchronize. Mobile device protection for such data is more refined, due to the portability of the device and absence of complete control. The mobile offline mode architecture should be implemented (see Sect. 3.5).

– Additionally, it is suggested:

1. Perform re-encryption on a server once a week. Use separate keys on a server and organize a key storage. Store master key with SS or on a flash drive/ smartphone with PIN.
2. Renovate attribute keys once a month.
3. Use PIN for mobile devices.
4. Send the renovated keys via protected channel.
5. Enhance reporting and analysis.

The system client workflow is summarized in Fig. 4.13.

The workflow for mobile client includes additional PIN checkup on every download or after 5 min of the device staying in idle.

The workflow for the server includes the key storage re-encryption and masterkey renovation. Once the user is deleted, the appropriate keys are renewed in case of ABE encryption. Due to the lack of space, these schemes are omitted.

Scenario 4.3: Bid Company

The properties of the solution:

1. Three or four levels of data confidentiality (open/protected/restricted/ confidential).
2. More than 500 people, several trusted administrators.
3. Information is accessible within a group or hierarchical access structure (if there are at least three subgroup levels).

The proposed security framework should provide the sufficient balance between usability and security. In many cases, it is enough to apply the above scenario. The additional security might include the following components:

1. *IMI: RA+AuthM+UDT/OTP or CP*: multifactor remote authentication with token generated from user data and device. It is often difficult to control the token security in the cloud environment that's why in a big company with many users it is necessary to implement an additional PIN checkup for every user. The PIN can be sent via SMS, email, or generated on a server side as a token and serve to prove the possession of a device by a user. The PIN should be entered by user on every synchronization request and after a certain period of device staying in the idle.
2. ACF:

   – *Policy setup*: Group hierarchy with three or four levels of confidentiality and files that are stored in clear on a server should be encrypted on a mobile device and encrypted on a client as well.
   – *KM and DE setup*: It is suggested to use ABE for the authorization support to avoid ambiguities in attribute setup as this is the only encryption method that provides the automatic attribute manipulation. The private ABE keys are protected with temporary AES key generated from the user token, PIN, and password [5]. If the requirements to the security system are very strict, it might be necessary to implement the encrypted key exchange protocol to protect the private keys [9]. The user token should be expiring.
   – *Revocation*: Once a user leaves a group, the keys of the ABE corresponding groups are renewed.

3. *Reporting*. It is suggested to report the file upload or download operations, key renewal, location change, and excessive tries. The analysis of all operations including DDoS attack analysis [12] and other suspicious activities should be performed. The reports should be prepared on a regular basis.
4. Component security:

   – *Server – Data at rest*: Server is protected by expiring administrator password. The encrypted storage is protected with AES encryption with separate key for each share, and the master key to the key storage is protected with administrator password. If the enhanced security is required, the SSS scheme is used to store the master key. The share of the master key is kept on a flash drive or protected by PIN of administrator's smartphone. *Data in transit*: Once the data is sent to client or mobile device, it is encrypted with AES and AES key is protected with ABE public key.

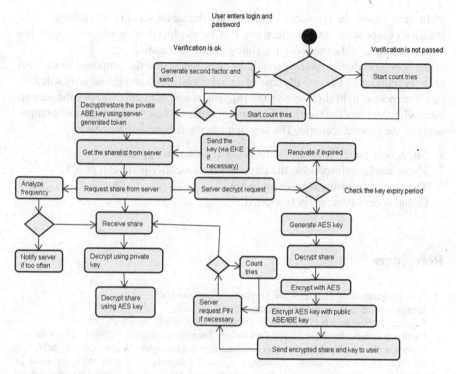

Fig. 4.14 The workflow for a big size storage client

- *Client – Data at rest*: Protected with the AES encryption, the key of AES is protected with the private ABE, and the ABE key is accessible only with a user token based on timestamp/secret sharing/EKE protocol. The share/private key/token belongs to the device/client computer so the data cannot be accessed from another computer and by another user. The PIN is verified after every share synchronization and after 5 min of user device in the idle. *Data in use*: The data modification is restricted. *Data leaving the premises*: Mobile offline protection is based on offline security architecture (see Sect. 3.5).
- Additionally, it is suggested:

1. Perform re-encryption on a server daily. Use separate AES keys on a server to encrypt the shares and organize a key storage. Use a strong method of protecting the master key, i.e., store all key or part of the key externally. Renovate authorization keys once a week.
2. Use PIN for all portable devices in a system.
3. Send the renovated keys via protected channel.
4. Enhance reporting and analysis.
5. Protect the client control zone and apply special policy for data leaving the client control zone.

The system client workflow can be summarized in Fig. 4.14.

In most cases, the resources of the system define its security level. Most of the security components and mechanisms can be deployed at nearly same cost but require the time and experience for configuration and testing.

To conclude this chapter, it should be mentioned that the proposed model and security framework became the base of an industrial cloud storage security solution, i.e., a corporate hybrid cloud storage [6]. The solution mainly follows the recommended guidelines for the third scenario and uses some mechanisms and components of the second scenario. The solution has the following properties:

1. The access policy is based on the two levels of share protection.
2. These levels correspond to the three levels of security perimeter policy.
3. The size of company is medium to big.
4. Group access structure is supported.

References

1. National Institute of Standards and Technology. www.nist.org
2. International Standardizaation Organization. www.iso.org
3. Schneier B, Ferguson N (2003) Practical cryptography. Wiley, New York
4. Common criteria for Information Technology Security Evaluation ISO\IEC 15408 (2005) Common criteria portal. http://www.commoncriteriaportal.org/cc/. Accessed 6 July 2016
5. ISO/IEC 18014 *Information technology – Security techniques – Time-stamping services* (2014) International Organization for Standardization. http://www.iso.org/iso/home/store/catalogue_tc/catalogue_detail.htm?csnumber=50678. Accessed 6 July 2016
6. Storgrid secure enterprise share and sync solution. http://www.storgrid.com/. Accessed 6 July 2016
7. Scoping SIG, Tokenization Taskforce, PCI SSC (2011) Information supplement: PCI DSS tokenization guidelines. PCI Security Standards Council. https://www.pcisecuritystandards.org/documents/Tokenization_Guidelines_Info_Supplement.pdf. Accessed 6 July 2016
8. Cloud Security Alliance (2010) Guidance for identity & access management: version 2.1. CSA Community. https://cloudsecurityalliance.org/guidance/csaguide-dom12-v2.10.pdf. Accessed 6 July 2016
9. Bellovin SM, Merritt M (1993) Augmented encrypted key exchange: a password-based protocol secure against dictionary attacks and password file compromise. ACM CCS'93: 244–250. doi:10.1145/168588.168618
10. Skyhigh research and reports (2015) What is cloud access security broker. In: Skyhigh Cloud University. https://www.skyhighnetworks.com/cloud-university/what-is-cloud-access-security-broker/. Cited 01 Feb 2016. Accessed 6 July 2016
11. Lawson C, MacDonald N, Lowans B (2015) Market guide for cloud access security brokers. Gartner research. http://www.gartner.com/technology/reprints.do?id=1-2RUEH70&ct=151110&st=sb. Cited 01 Feb 2016. Accessed 6 July 2016
12. Tenorio DF, da Costa JPCL, de Sousa Jr RT (2013) Greatest eigenvalue time vector approach for blind detection of malicious track. ICoFCS'2013: 46–51

Afterword

The presented two-level security system model and the step-by-step mechanism selection methodology break down the whole process of security framework implementation into the clear and easily verifiable procedures. The transparency of construction allows to perform the verification, testing, and optimization of the security components easily. Additionally, this book aims to help the technical specialists to understand the components of cloud security, including the typical threats and vulnerabilities.

For the needs of particular organization, the presented model can be specified with more details including the additional encryption options, attack analysis, and optimization steps. This book omits the detailed description of security testing and optimization.

The model and the complementary methodology were tested in the process of an industrial cloud storage solution implementation [1] and in the laboratory work on the methods of security modeling of the master's degree students at Belarusian State University specializing in applied informatics.

The authors expect that this book can be of use to academia as well as to the developers, analysts, and managers in the field of cloud storage security. It proposes a flexible component-wise approach to the security modeling based on the practical experience and approbation.

Reference

1. Storgrid secure enterprise share and sync solution. http://www.storgrid.com/. Accessed 6 July 2016

© The Author(s) 2016
T. Galibus et al., *Elements of Cloud Storage Security*, SpringerBriefs in Computer Science, DOI 10.1007/978-3-319-44962-3

Printed in the United States
By Bookmasters